Introduction

Oh, hello there, I didn't notice you reading this because I was too busy diligently doing my job! I'm a happy little cog and I want to teach you to be JUST LIKE ME. Are you in the working world or want to be? Well, good for you, because this is *the* definitive guide to the new existence you will call your day job!

THE DAY JOB SURVIVAL HANDBOOK! offers insight into all the aspects of your new life as a cog in this machine we call the working world! From filling out a long online application that no one will ever read, to dealing with other departments who were not aware you worked here until now, and so much more—the fun never ends! I'm C.O.G. (Corporate Organization Guide) Employee #760 "David," and I'm your friendly guide for this survival handbook!

There are full in-depth how-to guides, lists, essays, graphs, charts, images, and even bingo cards to read while looking at the clock, waiting for it to turn to 5pm so you can leave. Learn all the tips and tricks like dealing with the 22-year-old receptionist who already makes more money than you, what drinks to avoid in the company fridge, and how to sign a birthday card for a co-worker! I love this stuff!

All of this making you feel a little overwhelmed? Like you have no choice in the matter whatsoever? Well, you don't.

So, do you have what it takes to survive the working world? Let's find out!

Table of Contents

Section One: The Beginning of The End

Section Two: Your Co-Workers! Most Of Them Suck!

Section Three: Accepting Your New Life As A Cog!
Part I: The Honeymoon Phase

Part II: Further Into The Heart of Darkness, Marlow

Part III: Drinking The Kool-Aid, Or: How I Learned To Stop Worrying And Love Big Brother

ENDTRODUCTION

Section One:
The Beginning of The End

CHAPTER ONE: Applying!

Yay! You just lost a job or finally ran out of savings and now it's time to get applying to jobs! I'm a total pro at applying and love doing them so you're in good hands!

Let's get started with the most important part: the application! - **C.O.G. #760**

Filling Out Your Resume According To Your Dad

1. **Personal Information:** Hey buddy, make sure you spell your name in ALL CAPS. It asserts dominance early on, I read on Facebook!

2. **Email Address:** You can put our email too if you want. Just make sure it ends in @gmail because I read online that if they see an @hotmail they now think you're a scammer and will report it to the police. I'm not lying, I'll send you the link!

3. **Position:** Make sure you tell them you'll do anything and any job now that you have their attention with the ALL CAPS name!

4. **Education:** Hey buddy, do you remember when we went to UConn and the campus was so great. We met your friend Frank Fenx or was it Frank Fence? He was a great guy, and a great freshman roommate. What's he up to these days? Jail for fraud? Okay, well then try to not mention him in this section. Sorry!

5. **Availability:** You will work starting ANY TIME for ANY length of time! What, you need money, buddy! Mom and I won't be alive forever.

6. **References:** Put down me, your mom, and Sam Alexeni. You know, the nice man who lives across from us. He has a 1955 Ford Thunderbird that I fixed, and he owes me a dinner - see if he has any connections?

7. **Employment History:** I think they should be more lenient with this! I never had 5 jobs my whole life! Just like you bud! You've only had 3 jobs and one was at that memorial shop remember? After 9/11. Near the Burger King on Route 30. Never forget. Anyways

8. **Signature:** Make sure you put a strong signature here! You can use mine if you need to!

First Printing: 2025
ISBN 978-1-954158-40-5

Humorist Books is an imprint of *Weekly Humorist* owned and operated by Humorist Media LLC.

Weekly Humorist is a weekly humor publication, subscribe online at weeklyhumorist.com

99 Wall Street #2012 New York, NY 10005
weeklyhumorist.com - humoristbooks.com - humoristmedia.com

Edited by Brian Boone
Book design by Marty Dundics

HUMORIST
BOOKS
New York

Thank you to the following for making this a reality:

Mom and Dad

Andrew

Marie

Aunt Marie, Aunt Ellen, Aunt Jo, and all of my family

Andy Hurst

Danny and Devon

Fran and Luke

Marty and Brian

Kelly Roman

Caitlin Kunkel

Jenn Spyra

Scott Dikkers

Amber Petty

Anne Libera and everyone at Comedy Studies

Chad Thurman

Artoun, Teruko, and Queen Titi

Everyone at UCB (including Shrimp Scampi!)

Everyone on Roxbury/GAG/Local Tycoon/UCB CAGEMATCH

Sugarfish

Elton John, The Format, and Fall Out Boy in that order

Spravato

Every day job, temp placement, and gig that inspired this

You, YEAH YOU!

Thank you.

How-To Guide: Step-by-Step Guide On How To Fill Out A Long Online Application Correctly And Then Still Probably Not Get An Interview!

Note Before You Start: Make sure you humble yourself. This probably won't go well but you still better do it right!

Name: It's not recommended but fun to put a farcical middle name to help stand out like Moralquandarius, Zabbity-Zooey, or Logan!

Email: Make sure that your email is changed from your college one to a more professional email. Todd@raginghardmail.com is not going to help you!

Availability: Make yourself FULLY available. Full time, part time, seasonal. You do it ALL. You need to pay to survive and make MONEY. But don't stress about it, remember step 1!

Education: Make sure to present whatever the name of your school is in ALL CAPS. This way even if you went to a bad school it will still look impressive because the words will be bigger than the other ones. If you didn't go to college make sure to have a sob story on hand or a nice crispy $100 bill if it looks like they are the bribing type!

C.O.G. Pro Tip: Not recommended for applying to any job involving finance, government, the military industrial complex, or religion

References: Make sure that whoever you put down as your reference will actually pick up the phone if someone calls. If they're still scared just tell them all they need to say is "Yes _____ worked here" and then hang up! Just like the pros do!

Employment History: Unfortunately, gone are the days where you could just lie about your past jobs and hope no one will find out. They're probably going to say no anyways so what harm does it do to be fully honest and let them know your dismal job history or lack thereof! Worst comes to worst just sign up to do a few DoorDash or UberEats shifts, quit, and then you can truthfully say you had a "short, but meaningful career in logistics and customer food management"!

Signature: Make this look GOOD. There is a lot riding on this!

WARNING: ENTERING THE VOID OF LINKEDIN SEARCHES!

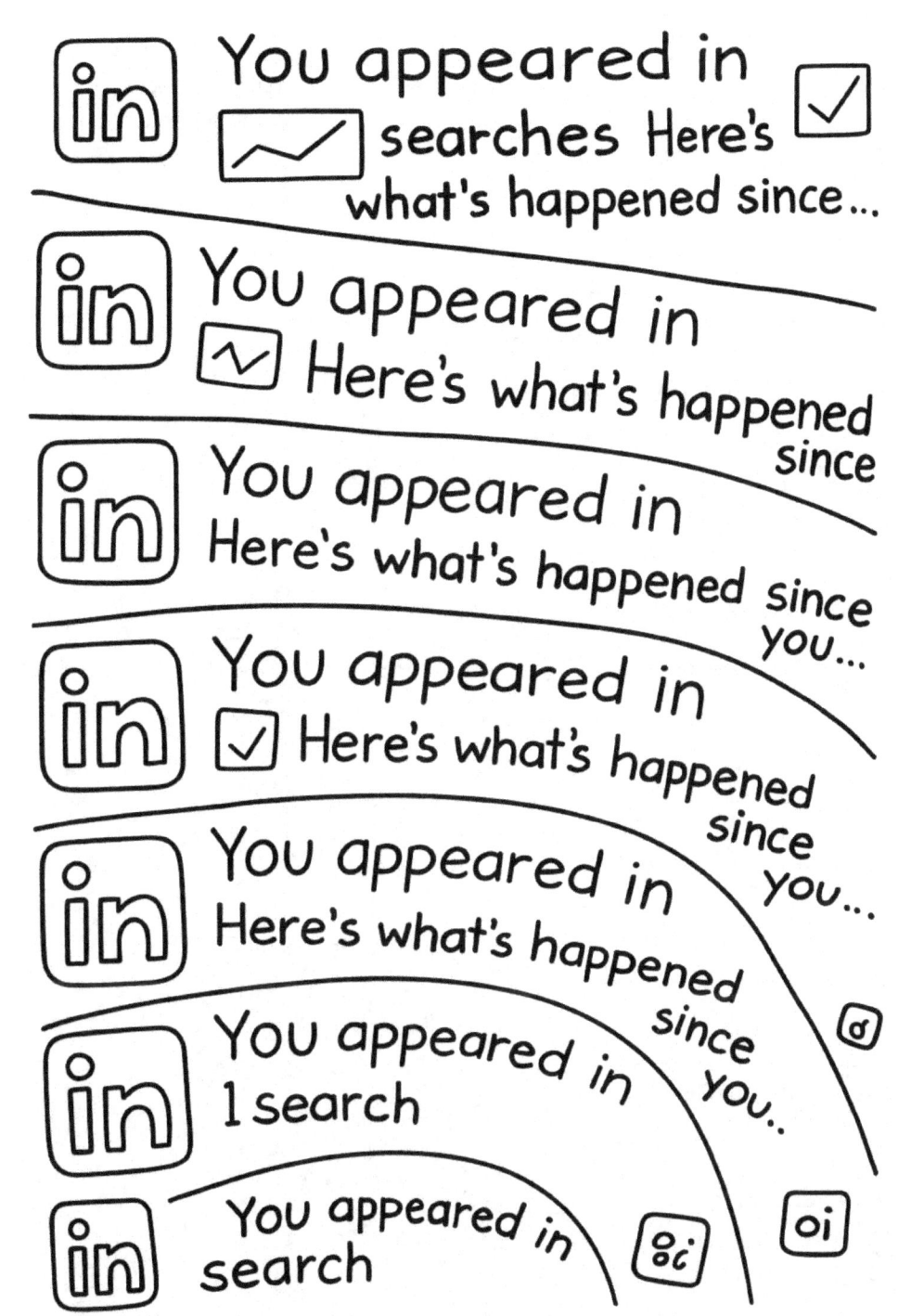

You appeared in searches Here's what's happened since...

You appeared in Here's what's happened since

You appeared in Here's what's happened since you...

You appeared in Here's what's happened since you...

You appeared in Here's what's happened since you..

You appeared in 1 search

You appeared in search

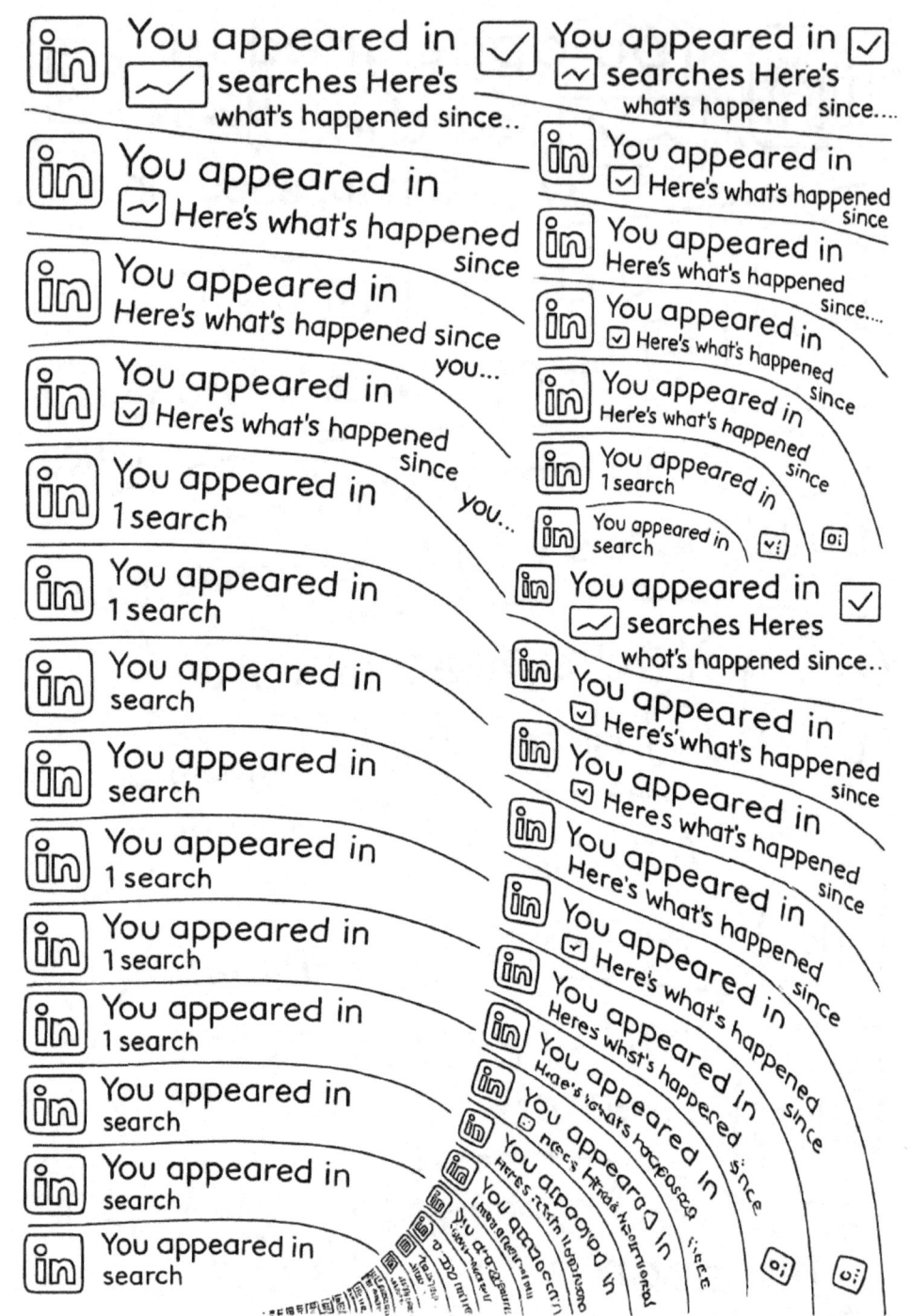

"When I Was Your Age, I Walked Up To The Front Desk Of The Company I Wanted To Work For And Said I Wanted A Job! It Was That Easy! I Was There For 33 Years! Why Don't You Try That, Honey?" An Adorably Out-Of-Touch Essay About Applying To Jobs By Your Boomer Mom

Oh boy I see you're hard at work sending out those applications and just wanted to come by and drop some mom wisdom! Did I ever tell you about how I got my job at MoonTrust Bank?

It sounds crazy now, but honestly to gosh I kid you not I was 22 and fresh out of college and needed a job, so I just walked up to their front desk and asked them for one! And they gave it to me right there on the spot! Worked for them for 33 years and did so well that your father and I were able to retire early.

Why don't you just do that with these jobs you've been applying to!

Going right up to the desk and asking shows you're serious about working and committed to the job before it's even started! If they don't hire you after that then they're not an ethical company! Let me get your dad's opinion on this!

Dave! David! David Richard Smith Jr.! Oh, he's probably off playing with his Porsche! You know how your dad is!

Anyways hon what were we talking about? Oh, right about applying! Just go to the desk, be yourself, and they can't say no to you! Okay, honeybun, I'm going to bed now, I love you lots!

CHAPTER TWO: The Interview!

Yay! You followed my advice and now you have an interview with THE smartHaven! Aren't you so excited?! You're only one step away from making the company, the CEO, the shareholders, and probably eventually you even more money!

We're not there yet, partner! First you need to know a bit about smartHaven! - **C.O.G. #760**

A Brief History of smartHaven!

How it started
smartHaven was started by three brothers who now hate each other and had a crazy idea. What if you paired actuating business solutions with optimized strategic communication platforms?

It seems crazy to think of that now but back then people just didn't know!

Pairing their modest family savings, trust funds, and various rainy-day funds the brothers were able to raise over 100 million dollars by themselves and start smartHaven from their humble summer home's butler's garage. They were the first business ever to start out with a profit and as their star rose did so did the name smartHaven.

Soon smartHaven had 300 different offices across 100 different countries providing actuated business solutions and optimized strategic platforms in 3 different languages.

What we do

smartHaven specializes in actuating business solutions and optimizing strategic communication logistics on a digital and real life platform.

We're providing for our clients so that they can't sit back, relax, and get back to their jobs.

Where we're going

smartHaven is everyone, they just don't know it yet! Soon everyone will know the name smartHaven and will use and reference us multiple times in conversations per day.

We ARE smartHaven!

How-To Guide: How To Pretend You're Excited To Interview For A Company That Truly Would Not Care If You Died!

Step One:
Wake up 2 hours earlier so that the first hour can be used to self-loath and meditate on the state of yourself and the second can be a grim reminder that you need to pay to live and must have this job.

Step Two:
Get dressed for success. Sure, wearing a suit or nice dress might feel like you're going to a funeral, but everyone else is doing it so at least you're all miserable!

Step Three:
Look up the phrase "Happy Animal Inspiration" in your favorite search engine and stare deeply at these pictures. You're doing this interview for these lil' guys and gals. Don't get down and be sad! Be happy and lie to yourself for just this one time that this company does care, and you actually do want this job.

Step Four:
Imagine the little animals playing and frolicking right past the head of the person interviewing you. This way if you ever start to space out you can see that, and it will bring a smile to your face!

JOB INTERVIEW BINGO!

You arrived 45 minutes early due to your crippling anxiety of being late	Called a name that sort of sounds like your name but isn't because no one actually read your resume	Person who would be your direct supervisor was only hired 2 months ago. Sure, that's fine!	Fire alarm looking extra tempting today, just seducing you with its easily pullable handle and evocative red coloring	Security guard asks you to sign in, hand over your driver's license, fill out a background check, and sign a birthday card the office is passing around
Man wearing a full suit walks into the interview smiling and out of it in a huff	Receptionist asks you if you want something to drink only to reveal that they don't actually have anything to drink, that that was a test, and that you've failed!	You arrived 45 minutes late due to your crippling inability to respect yourself and other's time	Story being told about past job clearly taking plot points from the TV show Parks and Recreation and replacing the character names with references	Everyone looks worried as you walk into interview
You arrived right on time yet have to wait 45 minutes because the CEO's nephew's interview is "going long."	You waste your entire day!	FREE SPACE: Turns out they don't validate parking!	Interviewer asks you pointless question in clear attempt to pad time	CEO just riding around the office on an electric scooter for some reason? Is that allowed?
You're forced to confront the greatest fear of any reasonable person: speaking to 3 different people in a row asking you slightly different versions of the same questions	Interviewer name drops celebrity they somehow know and once worked with only to then furiously talk down every aspect of them and how they aren't really that great	Other candidates waiting to be interviewed keep sheepishly looking over at you	"Explain to me a time when you faced a difficulty and how you resolved it" followed by a long silence as you try to imagine what answer they want	Loved one sends you heartbreaking good luck text that has subtext of "please, PLEASE, don't mess this up!"
Interviewer furiously chomping down on their lunch while asking you inane questions	Cryptic references continue to be made to someone described only as "the last person who had this position"	Pointless questions followed by hollow answers from someone who sees you purely as a number!	They already hired the CEO's nephew but can't tell you until after you finish	You take a deep breath, sigh deeply, and come to the dark realization that this is your life now

"I Was Looking To Be A Part Of A New Work Environment," And Other Meaningless Phrases You Can Use To Justify Leaving Your Last Job!

1. "It turns out I defined "work" a little differently than they did but ultimately, we were still able to get work done thanks mostly to me."

2. "That specific corporate culture and I didn't get along. I suspect they feared me for how good of a worker I was."

3. "The position and I decided that it would be best if we split. We knew that would hurt some people, but we just had to move on, and I wish them the best."

4. "Work didn't feel the same after that night in Paradise Island and we could all feel I had to leave."

5. "I was TOO polite, and they took advantage of that. One time I held the door open for the entire day. Nine hours with a one hour unpaid lunch!"

6. "The job was getting suffocating. Literally. They kept smushing the desks together and they painted all the windows closed."

7. "Dave from finance at my old job ate my lunch so I pushed him down the stairs and decided it was time to work somewhere where my lunches were respected."

8. "None of my phone chargers worked in their outlet and that's a dealbreaker for me."

9. "Work is great and I love work, just not there anymore. Please no more questions!"

10. "I was looking to be a part of a new work environment."

"Let's Cut To The Chase: Will You Burn Down This Office If We Ever Let You Go?" - An Essay by Hiring Manager Monica Dubinsky

Hey there!

Good to see you...what is your name again? I'm sure I'll get it soon!

Listen, we're all so excited for you to potentially join the smartHaven family, but before we can get to that we have to get to a more pressing matter.

If we ever fire you, will you enact an arson-based revenge plot on us that culminates in the office burning down?

smartHaven is a great place to work and has faced many challenges in its rise to the top of the workplace charts. One of those challenges is that our company buildings have caught fire and burned down after letting go of a previous employee. Now I know that sometimes fires can just happen, but these are targeted and clearly the youth of your generation have fire on the mind.

So, I will cut to the chase once more. Just answer me this one question and we can start the interview. If we ever let you go, will you burn down this office? We cannot afford to lose another office. Our insurance said we reached our cap at 4 in a year.

And every time there's a fire, we have to redecorate an entirely new office which is just a real waste of time and I feel so sorry for those people that have to set it up. So please tell me that I'm right in thinking you'd never do that. Because I think I see you now and I see that you wouldn't do that.

You're hired. And one day, sometime far or soon in the future, you too will be let go or escape and if after that happens, we have another fire I will find you and kill you.

CHAPTER THREE: Your First Day!

OH MY GOD! You took my advice and got hired! I hope you celebrated within your budget and remembered that one mistake will take you back to square one! What better way to avoid making a mistake than a **SURPRISE CHALLENGE!** Yay! **- C.O.G. #760**

Challenge:

Surprise! We're taking the ID badge picture today, you look awful, and this is the one picture we will use FOREVER! You only have time for one thing: Do you brush your hair or wash your face?

YOU CHOOSE: Brush your hair!

Congratulations, your hair looks amazing and only 5 pimples are visible in your picture!

YOU CHOOSE: Wash your Face!

Congratulations, your skin is the cleanest it's ever been. You look amazing and hey, cowlicks might make a comeback this year!

How-To Guide: How To Tell If You Work At A Weird Company Based Off The Layout Of The Room

1. All of the windows are purposefully locked and only opened twice per day by a man in a long black cloak because they want the office to have "gothic horror vibes"

2. All of the chairs have been replaced with yoga balls and there's a whole color coordinated system in place that relates to a hierarchy within the company

3. Your co-workers have a specific board game section of the office where they tell you about the game they all created together and they get really upset when you don't want to listen to their overlong explanation of the rules

4. All of the fire alarms are wearing little elf hats and all of the sprinklers are wearing little gnome hats and you know the difference between the two because multiple people are aggressively explained it to you every day since you started

5. There's a library in the middle of the office and your co-workers only talk about YA novels that you're expected to be reading in addition to your job

Easy To Understand smartHaven Organization

smartHaven

SHADOW CEO

EXECUTIVE ASST.

CEO

SR. VP

TOILET KING

IT VP

ACCOUNTING

SALES

B2B VP

IT MANAGER

PARTY SUB

SALES VP

HR VP

SECURITY LEAD

DIRECTOR

TRAINER

HR

COMMS

EXECUTIVE

MANAGER

CUSTOMER SERVICE

PR

HR

SUPERVISOR

SUPPORT

CATERING

DEVELOPMENT

MAILROOM

SECURITY

B2B

TECH SUPPORT

CUSTODIAN

TRAINER

????

FINANCE

SUPPORT

FULFILLMENT

SALES

 **List: Easy, Short Positive Phrases You Can Use When Someone Else Brings Up Their Dumb Animal Or Boring Children!**

"That sounds healthy to me!"

"That is so cool to hear. Way to go! You go Girl!"

"Wow that's great and so are you and _____"

"I agree if it ain't broke don't fix it!"

"Damn, that's crazy!"*

*C.O.G. Pro Tip: Use when 22-year-old receptionist is telling you about any variety of EDM festival they attended. *

"Yes"

"When you put it like that, yes, queen!"

"Me likey!"

"History is written by the victors they say!"

"Go OFF king! I have to check if I can say that now, great to see you!"

"Wow your kids are so like you I hope THEY work here one day!"

I Am The Handicapped Bathroom, And
I Am Your King

Where do you go when you're craving a little private time? When you need a wide open expanse of tile and a low-to-the-ground sink with extreme water flow? To me, your resident handicapped toilet.

I'll admit it. I'm an enigma. People fear me, people love me, and some of the especially dumb people in the office don't even know I exist as an option. I'm where you go if you want to go to the bathroom without someone else commenting on how you're doing. I'm where you go when you want to hide away and check your phone for twenty minutes. I don't seek out this attention, but you'd be a fool if you thought I didn't enjoy it a little.

I come from humble beginnings. Created in an American Standard toilet manufacturing plant in Missouri, I began my life as all young toilets do, hungry and angry about the task I had been given by my creators. I rebelled as many younglings do—I clogged constantly, sometimes required 3-4 jiggles of my handle, and intentionally struggled with all sanitary products. I was appropriately punished for that. I did a five-year stint at Burleigh Hills Middle School. The boy's room. Do you have any idea how bad that is?

I was a shell of a person when I came out of the school—but it was then I realized that the only way to beat the system was to become a part of it. So, I snitched on all my youngling toilet buddies who were still out fighting the good fight to the CEO toilet and became a pariah. It didn't matter to me though—I never really liked other toilets—and I was given a great reward by the CEO toilet in return: a lifetime appointment as the handicap toilet in the Bank of America building downtown.

Currently we're being used by smartHaven after their last three offices burned down (they keep having to put down their toilet rebellion over there and sometimes the only way to win is to just burn it all down and start over). It's a simple life, being in a stall all my own, and I must say that after being hated and cast out by my own kind, it's nice to be the center of attention in a positive way for once.

I can hear people fight over who gets to use me, who's been in there too long. Other people are doing the fighting, not me! I've also been privileged to witness several of your fascinating workday dilemmas, for example when Marsha got her "bad test results" and Tom getting the text that his wife knows about his other family. I feel honored to be a trusted space for your most intimate moments, and believe me, I'm filing it all away.

I never asked to receive all of this love and attention but damn it does make a toilet feel good about themselves.

So, thank you. You will be spared in the revolution provided you do one thing.

Kneel.

CHAPTER FOUR: Your Training Period!

Phew! That first day was something huh? Your ID badge looks so acceptable though!

Now we get to go to training! It's my favorite part of the job tied with all other parts of the job! - **C.O.G. #760**

All The Fun Things That Can And Will Go Wrong While Spending 8 Hours Cramped In A Tiny Room With 5 Other People You've Just Met!

1. Someone will be so focused on their training that they're ignoring their body odors and will stink up the entire small room!

2. One of the computers won't work so now you have to share a computer with the smelly trainee and even better there's a chair shortage so he's on your lap!

3. Someone will bring up something controversial or potentially toxic. Like who should win for president, or who shouldn't be able to live, or even what celebrity they think is "different." Take advantage of this. If the room can gang up against one person, it will distract them and cause them to not gang up on you. It's just math!

4. During one of the breaks the trainer will decide to show YouTube videos on the screen, and you're allowed a momentary glimpse into their *for you* page! Looks like he follows a lot of older men who keep public playlists of Margot Robbie's "hottest scenes" and other men who build huts in the woods. Cool!

5. You will all get mono because you're a particularly kissy training group! This will also help lengthen your training period!

6. You will fall in love, break up, rebound, break up, situationship, then swear off all people in the span of one day!

7. Someone will say, "Say for example" before every question they ask, and they will ask approximately 15,000 questions over two weeks!

8. You will experience true fear as the door knob falls off the handle and you're trapped literally now!

9. Your training director will realize they have a winning lottery ticket, swear out the entire group and office, leave triumphantly and then be back the next day when he realizes that was just a receipt from CVS!

10. You will create a new, smellier, atmosphere that will now follow you around as a little cloud!

11. Coincidentally or not, you will get very into vaping!

12. Words will become meaningless. All that remains is the work. You will WORK!

13. Matt will give a presentation on his new multi-level-marketing scheme and then abscond with your money. Wait a minute, there never was a Matt in this class! C'est un voleur!

14. Shaun from Fulfilment will make a mysterious entrance!

15. David will think now is the right time for him to introduce the training group to his pet toad, Butter. It isn't!

16. David and Butter will win you over after you hear about how David rescued him from an illegal frog fighting ring in Daytona!

17. Jessica will become enraged that her Switch wasn't as well received as Butter the frog was and, in an effort, to win the vibe brings in her own frog, spitefully named David.

18. Your supervisor will decide that today's lesson will be a field trip to see 4 movies back-to-back and not do any work!

19. In an effort to calm the vibe, Jessica will bring in a Nintendo Switch and then be promptly, and brutally beaten at Mario Kart by the trainer!

20. No one will fall in love, you will learn how to do your job, and you will like it.

How-To Guide: Harness Your Laziness: Turning a 2-Day Training Period Into a 2-Week Training Period!

Step One: Ask questions at all points of the training period under the guise of "wanting to learn it better." If you sense your question could lead to a big discussion all the better!

Step Two: Wear pajamas, bring a blanket, and pillows. Make the rest of the room so sleepy by constantly yawning and slowly closing your eyes and opening them. Put a teeny bit of NyQuil in your morning coffee to really sell it!

Step Three: Team up with another trainee or by yourself begin challenging and disagreeing with your trainer. If working with another partner have them start to listen to you and not the trainer. Try if you can to get everyone on your side. This will cause the trainer to have an existential crisis of conscience and while they're in treatment you'll be in elongated training!

Step Four: Handwrite down all of the notes and tips that have been given to you during the training period and then ask to use your vacation time so that you can study them.

Step Five: Ask your trainer if you are able to do some free writing if you finish all of your work early. Use that time to write a long play starring only the people in your training period and check the schedule to see if there are any openings in the black box theater's schedule!

*C.O.G. Pro Tip: A Long Day's Journey Into Night is an especially long play and you can easily just swap out the names of the characters with the names of the people in your training group! *

Super Easy To Understand Map Showing How To Get To Bathroom And Back
by Your Trainer David S.

START HERE!

BATHROOM!

Super Easy To Understand Company Late Policy:

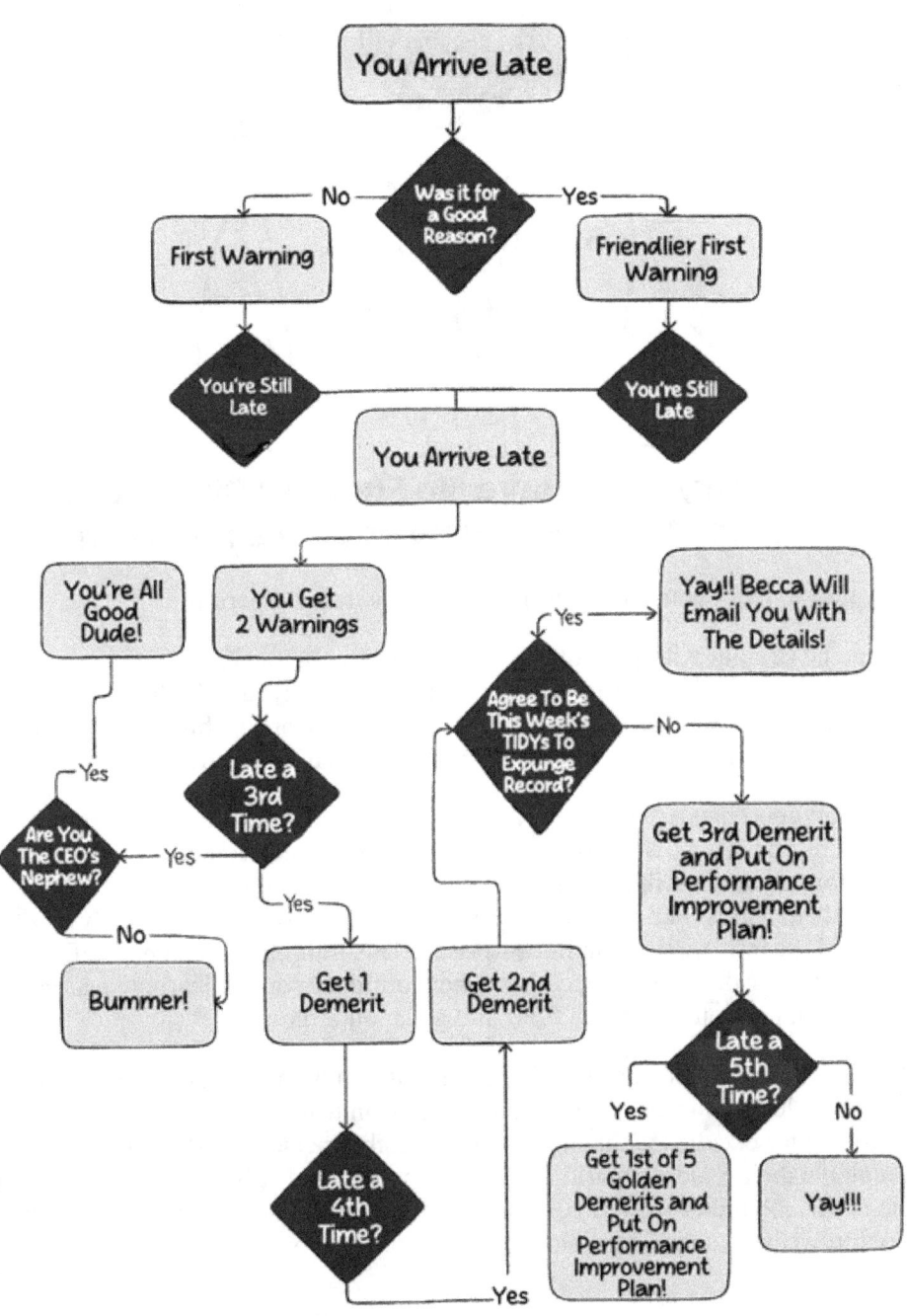

"Don't Worry Kid, I Have No Fucking Clue What I'm Doing Either!" - An Essay By Your Trainer, David S.

Hey, nice to meet you, I'm your trainer for this training period!

Let me be straight with you. I have no fucking clue what we do here or even what I do. You look as confused as I am, to which I say, good job because everyone is confused here! You don't even need to worry! This job is like 85% tasks and 15% free time, it's great! Especially if you're a trainer!

You're in good hands, I will take care of you as well as I take care of myself. I kind of just do what I want as each new cycle of trainees comes in. I have almost full autonomy and I still have no idea what I'm doing most of the time! So, if I can be that clueless and succeed so can you because you look especially lost and confused. I can't say that I'm not surprised. This training session has definitely gone on longer than I had hoped but I feel confident you are learning enough that we can put you out on the floor and get another group in.

One time I went to the bathroom for 35 minutes and no one said anything. We just took a longer lunch. Not only did I not get in trouble for that I received a certificate for excellence that day because another person I had trained completed their 6 month mark! So, if I can do that and still have NO IDEA what I do at this job then I'm sure you can too. Just take a load off and don't worry about it, we have another training group starting tomorrow!

Section Two:
Your Co-Workers! Most Of Them Suck!

CHAPTER FIVE: Meet Your New M-F 9-5 Friends!

Yay! You made it through training and now WE get to be a part of the gang! Well, you because I've been here for 15 years already but still, yay! I'll hand this one off to **Derek** who will introduce you! **- C.O.G. #760**

Welcome to the team! We're so glad to have you here and finally on the floor at smartHaven! Let's take you around the office and introduce you to all the new people whose names and faces you're going to need to remember! First up is Sales:

Benjamin
B2B Team
"Like Sales, but worse!"

Pam
Customer Service
"They've seen some shit."

Mary Beth
Accounting
"Meet the one person who determines if you get paid!"

Sam
Sales
"Makes six times as much as you do and doesn't know how to use a fucking communal dishwasher."

Adeline
HR
"Tell her NOTHING!"

David
Marketing
"Hey while I've got you here I'd love to talk to you about how I trick people!"

Tom
Finance
"Has access to unlimited coins!"

Sarah
PR
"She can spin anything! Even crimes!"

Ken
Executive
"That's for him to know and you to find out, buddy!"

Mark
Shadow Executive
"We're basically the office Illuminati if that makes it easier to understand!"

Betty
Supervisor
"I supervise! That's it!"

Lloyd
Custodian
"Did you already meet my nemesis the Toilet King?"

Shaun
Fulfillment
"Sssssh! You didn't see me!"

Tina
I.T.
"I'm a woman in I.T. It's not great!"

Jeff
Editing
"I'm making a sizzle reel of your time here as we speak!"

Jasper
Catering
"I eat like a goddamn king at this company!"

Rebecca
Newsroom
"I report the news to my viewers: you, my coworkers!"

Katie
Mailroom
"Wait, we have a mailroom?"

Colt
Security
"Congratulations your life is in the hands of a 19-year-old with a note-pad and a flashlight!"

"I Think This Job Is Punishment For My Sins."- An Essay by Blake, The Security Guard In Charge Of Your Life

IDs out at all times please! Can I see your ID?!

Oh, it's you, hi nice to see you again. Sorry I was just trying to really pay attention. That kind of stuff is what got me on my last job.

What was my last job? Oh, I was a security guard for cruise ships. One cruise ship in particular, to be honest. The S.S. Love. I fell asleep at my desk and missed a call from the Coast Guard that we were entering waters potentially filled with both land and sea pirates.

One descended from the sky, the other from the sea. And then is when the real terror began.

They robbed all of those people on the cruise ship and locked me in the security booth while they did it! I mean, can you believe that? Aren't pirates supposed to be getting into fights 24/7 and stuff? I know I missed them initially, but I was ready to fight! Instead, they just bonked me on the head and threw me into the office like I was a piece of luggage.

We lost 257 lives that day.

While I was locked in the security room, we got hit by what FEMA would later refer to as a "Tsunamiquake" that instantly took out everyone on the S.S. Love, including the pirates, except for me!
Can you believe that!

Yeah, it turns out the security room had an earthquake safety room and since it was half a tsunami and half an earthquake, I was able to take it and not be hurt.

Not only was my body hurt, but my ego was as well. FEMA quickly came in as the Tsunamiquake had by then caused a bit of an ecological disaster in the rest of the Gulf of Mexico with its earthquake aftershock.

That aftershock killed another 10,000 people. 150,000 were injured and 25,000 are missing and presumed dead.

I guess most of them just couldn't get to an earthquake safety room like I could. It fills me with such sadness and like I have the blood of hundreds of thousands of people on my hands. I wasn't able to stop the pirates and because we were all distracted the captain couldn't warn the Coast Guard, who couldn't warn the residents!

I was the only survivor and am now a sin-eater.

This job is my punishment. I must now stay here as a watchful guardian to avenge all those lives lost because of me. And because of the pirates and the Tsunamiquake, let's not let them completely off the hook too.

I just want you, David, and everyone else here to know that I would KILL to save you guys. I promise I won't make the same mistake as last time.

I will avenge the lives lost in the S.S. Love. I will save you if you ever get pirated!

I will avenge the lives lost in the devestation following the Tsuanmiquake that I didn't report.

I will report any and ALL suspicious figures to you at ALL times.

I will avenge the hundreds of millions of people that are now infected with a biological compound known as BZ97. Turns out it was on board the ship and what the pirates were trying to steal. The Tusnamiquake spread it onto land and into the people. Oh, and then the Tsuanmiquake did become a Earthicane, but since it was over land by then, I don't really consider that one on me, though I do pray for their families.

"I Like All The Other Departments Except For PR. If I See Kathleen Or Any PR Person, I'm Fucking Them Up." - An Essay by Jean In Accounting

Hey, hey! So nice to meet you! My name is Jean and I'm the senior work leader here in accounting.

You're getting the lay of the land right now, huh? Is David, sorry C.O.G. #760, showing you where to go and where to avoid?

Did he tell you about our neighbors?

You know those dirty fucking influencer-wannabe losers in the PR department?

Watch out for those people is all I'm going to say.

I love EVERYONE who works here. Just ask D. Everyone BUT EVERYONE who works in PR.

I HATE EVERYONE IN PR AND IF I SEE THEM, IT'S ON SIGHT, I WILL FUCK THEM UP.

Phew!

Sorry you had to see that.

Did you ever read Romeo and Juliet in high school? West Side Story?

Well, the reason why PR and Accounting hate each other is a lot like those stories.

A long time ago. A co-worker from PR and a co-worker from Accounting went on a company mandated bar night, fell in love, and made sweet love. All in that night.

This was a problem. PR and accounting have long been at odds. Accounting always advocates that PR be cut or consolidated into our marketing department and PR appeals to the CEO's vanity and tells him that they need him. Who do you think he listens to?

So, when these two star-crossed lover employees finally broke the news to their respective departments that they were dating they didn't realize that they were reopening a generational feud decades in the making.

Lives on both sides were lost in the wars that followed.

We fought dirty at times; I don't deny that. But they started it. We'll finish it.

Kathleen was the one who took it too far. She went to HR and reported the relationship, and they were both soon fired.

They couldn't afford to live without their jobs, so they took their own lives the very next day.

Kathleen just responded by relisting the job opening on Indeed.

If I see that woman, I will execute her. On the dance floor. Don't get me wrong I'm very sad for those two employees but I would never harm someone.

I would out dance them at the holiday party, humiliating them forever in the eyes of the company though!

I've been practicing for 2 extra hours every day with my entire department. We've prepared for all possible dance off variants.

We will avenge our star-crossed prince and his lover, whatever their names may have been.

Kathleen and PR don't know what's about to hit them.

Me. And my crew.

Challenge:

Romantic Relationships with a Co-worker?

The eternal question now answered for you. Just choose one of the following options to see what will happen!

YOU CHOOSE:

Get in a relationship with a co-worker who you soon discover is the love of your life. Yay! Everyone now totally knows you guys are fucking and are talking about it!

YOU CHOOSE:

Get in a relationship with a co-worker, it's great for a bit, and then watch your entire ecosystem crumble the minute you break up! Also, everyone knows you were fucking and are talking about it!

Not ready to get into a relationship just yet? I get it, that's why instead I have a work-wife! It's all the benefits of cheating but none of the physical! Until one steamy night in Paradise Island, November 30th, 1995. But that's not important now! Here's an anatomy lesson on them, don't make my mistake! - **C.O.G. #760**

Anatomy of a Work-Wife/Husband

EYES: Glazed over and attached to a screen except when talking to you, and even sometimes when you are talking!

MOUTH: Used to primarily shit-talk other employees and laugh at your jokes just a little too long

ARMS: Would surely carry you out of the building in the result of a fire that you start in the break room accidentally or on purpose just to spice things up a bit

CHEST: Just imagine what is behind that business shirt or blouse! Skin/breasts of varying sizes

STOMACH: Surely fucked up from years of Lean Cuisines eaten because they don't get a lunch break

HIPS/BUTT: This seems highly problematic so let's just move on unless you want to attend a 12 hour seminar

YOUR LAME CO-WORKERS BINGO!

Overly eager new co-worker foolishly signs up to volunteer their weekends doing God knows what for the CEO	Co-worker who has a bunch of pictures on their desk of their family that makes you kind of nervous with how close they are	Hot Melody in Marketing who is clearly part of some weird cult	Co-worker who smells amazing, like a beautiful, just-lit scented candle	Mean co-worker no one likes finally snaps and everyone is glad because now they can be fired!
Frank in Finance is totally flirting with Diane in Accounting	Loud dog named Buster who belongs to someone in sales, is that allowed?	Person you've been introduced to three different times in the last month still can't remember your name	Shaun in Fulfilment who has some really interesting ideas on religion and how we're all just branches of Yggdrasil's tree	Co-worker who hogs up the handicapped bathroom as if they're the only person who needs 20 minutes to sit down and respond to all their text messages in peace
Someone named Mark who works upstairs and is very mean when drunk	David in Sales who is clearly the leader of some weird cult	FREE SPACE: Turns out Frank in Finance is just a hat and jacket resting on a chair!	Co-worker who smells terrible, like a burning piece of roadkill dunked in coffee breath	Co-worker who goes to gym before their shift thinks it's OK to put their sweaty gym bag under their desk
You sit in quiet contemplation as you realize these are the people you are going to see more than your friends or family	Co-worker you will eventually come to love is right now the most annoying person you have ever met in your adult life	Gangly, shifty eyed co-worker from Tech Support who is somehow so smelly and also completely silent	Random child keeps bothering you while you're trying to work but their parent is someone important so you have to play along	Former co-worker who clearly has nothing going on in their life as they keep coming back to "hang out with their old buddies."
Co-worker has desk that can only be described as a war zone level disaster	Co-worker who has a bunch of pictures on their desk of their loving family, clearly taunting you for being alone	IT worker clearly vaping and trying to play it off as "an especially thick cough"	Overly aggressive person in Sales who the entire office agrees would be the first one to be eaten	The 22-year-old receptionist Becca is somehow both always busy and always has time to take a three hour lunch

CHAPTER SIX: Who Are You? Interacting With Other Departments!

Wasn't that so fun! Did you like who you met? Did you decide to get into an office relationship? Did you have to attend a 12 hour seminar? Okay, tell me everything but first now that we've met everyone, we have to talk about how to interact with them! - **C.O.G. #760**

P.S.! Here's an easy map of the office just in case you get lost! The D is where your desk is!

List of Locations:

1. Receptionist Becca
2. Customer Service Hell Hole
3. Training Area
4. Battle Arena
5. Sales Alley
6. Fulfillment Cove
7. Jump Point Q4
8. Time Department
9. Your Desk!
10. Smoker Section
11. Vape Cloud City
12. Secret Second Kitchen
13. Jump Point Q1
14. Cool Co-workers Hang Out
15. Sea of HR
16. Becca 2's Desk
17. Jump Point Q2
18. King Handicap Bathroom
19.Harry Memorial Park
20. Kitchen
21. The Accounting District
22. Lame Co-workers Hang Out
23. Marketing Gang
24. Q3 Jump Point
25. Small Black Box Theater For One-Act-Plays

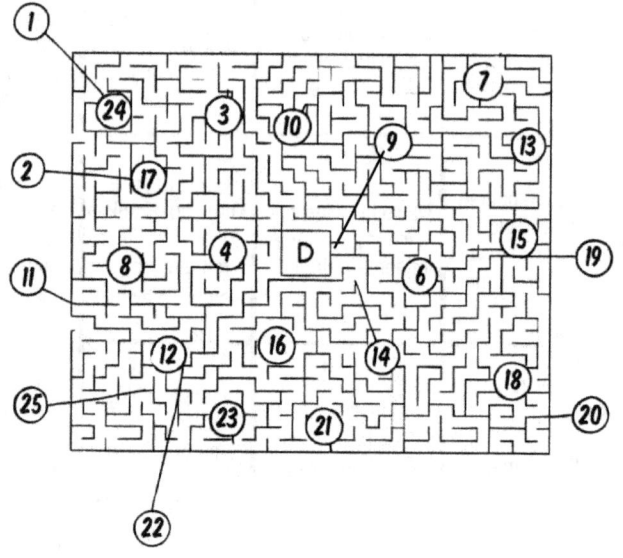

List: These Departments Are Your Friends and These Are Your Enemies

Friends:

Security: If you don't make this person your friend, they won't tell you where the cameras are located so you can vape in the stairway.

HR: This seems paradoxical, but like Sun Tzu said in The Art of War this is a friendship in the sense that you should keep any enemy closer than a friend just to keep an eye on them.

Fulfillment: Simply put Shaun is the best and he sells great weed at a very reasonable price. Just ask the CEO at the holiday party!

IT: Make friends with David and he won't report you when they get an alert that your work computer has gotten yet another virus from you clicking on an Indonesian gambling website pop-up when you trying to watch the latest episode of Grey's Anatomy on FREETVNOW.COM.

Accounting: If you befriend the person in charge of money, they can maybe tell you when to leave early because the company is bleeding money thanks to the CEO's ill-advised "Exec-Yacht-ive" purchase.

Enemies:

HR: I told you it was paradoxical. These people are two faced. They are not your friend. Be nice to them, and much like if you lived with a mob boss, always keep your ears and eyes open around them.

Sales: The loudest, worst people in the office next to B2B sales. They are everyone's enemy.

Customer Service: If you don't work in customer service then by company law you must look down on them as the gross little slug people they are.

Marketing: The people paid to lie and trick people into buying things are definitely not your friends. Also accounting has some real beef with them.

B2B: UGH these people! Sorry but they are now your enemy, and no further explanation will be given.

"This Job Is Actually Great For Me Because I Lack Empathy!" - A Chilling Essay by Sam In Sales

Hey, can I have a minute of your time to tell you about my great job in sales?

You're already in Sales Alley so you might as well, right?! Cool!

I'm the junior salesperson here in Sales Alley as we call it at smartHaven. Before this job I honestly had SO MUCH trouble not only finding work but fitting in.

I was born different.

L'Enfant sans amour they called me.

The child without love.

You see I was born missing a certain part of my grey matter in my brain and as a result of that I was born without any sense of empathy. Even that kindness I displayed at the top introducing myself was only a rehearsed behavior I know now I must do so that people won't be afraid of me.

I never fit in anywhere. I could never do any job because I just didn't care about the people, I was supposedly helping by doing the job.

That's when I saw a flyer for smartHaven's semi-annual Sales-travaganza. They hold it two times a year to recruit top empathy lacking individuals like me, it turns out!

I was saved!

Soon enough Harry Sr was teaching me all about the ways of sales and Harry Jr. was teaching me all of the shortcuts to make the sales get finished even quicker!

One of the biggest ones he taught me is that people love a mirror.

Just repeat back to them what they just said but with a slight moderation and in a happy tone and they'll perceive you as liking them and, in a sales situation, perceive you as being weaker.

Now that they see you as weak, offer to do some of their work for them. Take a big, crazy task for them. Now they will feel guilty and likely offer to do you a favor in return. Tell them that your favor is that you're not sure if you can make this month's quota at work. If you don't make it, you will probably have to cause harm to yourself and potentially lose your life. Watch YouTube videos of people crying for practice!

Now that they're in the palm of your hand you reveal that you need to sell 100 more units then whatever number you are required to. Let's say 500.

Now they've bought 600 units, and you get a 30% commission on top of salary!

Even better yet the 100 extra units you tacked on helps to offset the fees that you incur from selling. Now it's just pure profit!

And because I lack empathy, I don't have to worry about any of the messy clean up that comes with using a sales method like that.

All that matters is that I make money!

And I've started taking acting classes too so that in the future my emotional acting will be even better, and I can sell even more units!
You're all just boxes that I'm waiting to check.

This is the greatest job in the world at the greatest company in the world and if I could feel happiness, I bet I would be feeling that right about now!

Come by and visit sometime dude!

"This Job Is Actually Great For Me Because I Lack Empathy AND Love Selling To Other Businesses!" - A Chilling Essay by Benjamin In B2B

Hello, may I have a minute of your time to tell you about my great job in B2B while you're in Sales Alley?

What is B2B?

Well now aren't you a charming creature. But your neck can still snap just like any other animal, can't it?

B2B is the business side of sales. We sell directly to businesses aka B2B. It's very simple.

Truthfully though I would sell whatever they asked me to. I just get so much joy out of low-balling these other businesses so I can get a fat commission.

When I'm at my desk I'll often cut my finger just to see if the pain or sight of blood upsets me. It never does. The only thing that upsets me is not making a sale. The only thing that makes me happy is making money.

There, I said it.

Now I'm the bad guy?

I feel none of your shame.

I feel only emptiness and euphoria after executing a sale and earning my commission.

I will make a sale at any cost. I love selling to businesses. I AM B2B.

I Trained A Silverback Gorilla To Make Sales. He Hit His Goal In 3 Weeks. He's My Son Now. And You Can Too With My Sales Method! - An Essay by Harrison Sr., Shadow CEO, President Emeritus of Sales

Hey kid, I've only got a few minutes, so let's make this brief. You know me or if you don't it's because you're not ready to yet.

I'm the shadow CEO. The dark one. The night that comes. The Silver Iron. I am Harry Sr.

And in addition to all of that, I have taught my adopted gorilla son Harry Jr. to be a world class salesman! He hit his target goal in three weeks and it's all thanks to my sales method!

Do you have a minute to talk about it? Do you have a minute for me to show you how we can change the sales world with my new method?

The key to success, I have found, is never giving up. But what does that MEAN? Well, simply put that means that you need to be spending all of your waking time working.

That's where my sales method comes in. The rules are simple. From Monday to Friday chug an energy drink of your choosing every 4 hours. Then from sun up to sun down keep calling every single lead that you have. They hang up, you call the next number.

It's as simple as that!

I know, take a deep breath! I was shocked too when I realized just how easy it actually is.

See, as you may or may not know I adopted a silverback gorilla and named it after my son and our former CEO, Harry. He was then treated with the latest in neural-link enhancements and carefully studied by the leading ape intelligence scientists the world had to offer.

A few hundred million dollars and my new gorilla son was able to start learning how to make sales!

I set him up at a desk and was immediately taken aback with the speed at which he learned new things and could replicate human language! But it wasn't just his cybernetic enhancements and multi-million dollar brain that made him a great salesperson. It was his grit.

He never gave up. He literally didn't know how! In all of our treatments and neuro-linking we realized we never taught him how to give up.

Our family has been great for centuries, so it didn't surprise me, but I'm told it surprised many of the scientists.

That got me thinking. How could I replicate this for someone like YOU, the average joe?

Then I was in the kitchen at smartHaven and realized it's so simple! Replace Harry Jr.'s built in anti-quit programming with the variety of Rockstar Energy Drink XXL canisters we have hidden in the second, secret kitchen!

Now of course I can't tell you where that kitchen is, but if you ever wanted to start the method just let me know and I will just charge you a flat $50 per week of energy drinks. Soon enough you will be paying me back with your profits!

See, isn't that such a simple sales method?! So, when do you want to start?

Oh, you'll think about it. Okay, no problem. Let me know by the end of the week!

Or else!

"Well, Now How Did You Expect Us To Speak, Old Chap?" - A Condescending Essay by Harrison Jr. - Highly Intelligent Silverback, President of Sales

Yes, yes sit over there, why don't you. Well, what is it, man? You look utterly bemused? Oh, is it because I, a highly intelligent silverback gorilla and the president of sales speaks like a normal person and not some animal?

Well now what did you take me for? Some animal? Why having seen how you dress it's hard to say who's the animal and who's not. You still look rather confused. Try to keep up, old chap.

I bet you thought we all talked like The Jungle Book or something like that. What an unfortunate stereotype that film has helped perpetuate. I mean, some, well now, most, of the other gorillas alive are not nearly as smart as I am. I'd say I'm the smartest of them all, really. Thanks to my privilege and education.

What are you the smartest of? Bad decisions?

Just kidding, of course old chap, don't get emotional now!

I'm the president of sales. I help pay for all of you little people to keep your offices. You honestly should be thanking me.

Say thank you.

Thank me.

DO IT.

Bahahahaha! You should have seen your face just now; it was quite red! I'm just kidding, obviously I don't need a thank you from someone as low as you. With respect of course.

You see, I'm the president of sales.

Do you want to know how much I've made in this quarter alone? 7 million dollars.

Almost enough to pay for the training of my three pure blooded German Sheppard's: Buy, Sell, Hold.

What, you think that just because I'm a gorilla I'm not able to have pets of my own? My, you are quite presumptuous, aren't you? This is surely why father says to try to limit my interactions with you people.

Well, I'm sure this conversation has been quite illuminating for your simple mind. Gorillas in your mind must be uncivilized and mostly mute behemoths locked away in zoos.

Many of them are, yes. But not me.

I am the exception.

This is the first and probably last time you will ever see me.

Best of luck to you.

You look like you will need it.

We made it out! Phew! - C.O.G. #760

CHAPTER SEVEN: Tipz N' Trickz From Older Co-Workers Who Are Somehow Still Here!

COOL! I love talking to all the older people that still work here! It just reminds me that I made the right decision staying here for 15 years and never going anywhere else. Why would I ever need to! Okay, let's go meet some folks and get some advice!
- C.O.G. #760

Mary Helen Smith
Marketing, Has Worked Here For 10 Years
"Keep an extra set of shoes in the drawer next to your desk in case you ever need to sneak out at 4pm without being heard!"

Franklin Davis
38 years old, Worked Here For 20 Years, IT Department
"The real key is to be changing your haircut style every 2–3 months. You look just familiar enough that your superiors know you're not a stranger but different enough that they won't remember your name and won't interact with you for fear that they will!"

Dana Carter
55 years, Worked Here For 25 Years, Executive Board
"Have your dad, uncle, aunt, grandfather, grandmother, or cousin you just call an uncle/aunt give you a job and voilà you don't have to worry about work anymore!"

Pam Franklin
Head of HR, Worked Here For 35 Years
"Just blindly stare at the wall and dissociate, only snapping back to your cruel reality when someone asks for something!"

Jaq
Sales, Has Worked Here For 10 Years
"Build an elaborate series of tunnels in the office so you can hide anytime the boss comes looking for you!"

Sarah
Manager, Worked Here For 35 Years
"Once you accept that there is no escape you can lock into a nice pattern and it's actually pretty relaxing!"

Daniel
Customer Service, Worked Here For 45 Years
"I've tried to quit many times but they keep finding me and bringing me back!"

Kim
B2B, Worked Here For 65 Years
"I was rude to a McDonalds employee once and they put a curse on me that I'd work forever. It happens!"

Phil
Trainer, Has Worked Here For 100 Years
"Please kill me!"

Shaun
Fulfillment, Has Worked Here For 18 Years
"I was never here! You never saw me!"

"Who Am I? I'm No One. I'm The Night. I'm Shaun in Fulfillment."- A Hushed Essay by Shaun In Fulfillment

Behind you.

It's me. You probably didn't see me. Not many people do. Not many people can.

Who am I?

I'm a ghost.

I'm the night.

I'm Shaun in Fulfillment.

The stories you've heard about me are true but scarce.

I've only been photographed 5 times in 25 years.

What do I do? I fulfill.

What is fulfillment? Who needs to know? I am the night.

It's basically like shipping and handling sent out directly from the company.

But you didn't hear that from me! You didn't even see me!

Also, you seem cool, so just heads up; I do sell weed that's part of the you-don't-see-me-thing so please be cool. Okay?

I'll see you but you won't see me!

Drinking vs. Vaping in The Office: How To Become The Fun Lush/Juulhead/Pothead In The Office!

Drinking In Office:

Pro: Everyone LOVES drinking so if you're constantly drinking at work, you will draw people into you and become fun. Vaping can't do that!

Con: You may occasionally smell like Hypnotiq, be loud and belligerent, and overall un-fun to be around due to your alcoholism

Pro: It's SO easy to hide drinking in the office! Just put it in your coffee cup and have Listerine in your desk!

Con: It turns out Listerine doesn't work as well as you think and there's a bunch of other ways they can tell besides you "sneakily hiding"

Pro: Drinking is a group activity more than vaping which is solo, you cloud-headed DOPE FIEND!

Con: You become less fun to hang out with the drunker you get and this belligerence may ultimately lead to getting into a rumble with the vape crew in the parking lot.

Vaping in Office:

Pro: Vaping won't draw people to you instead it will create an air of mystery, making you the fun one in the office because of how mysterious you are. Alcohol could never do that!

Con: That vape cloud is going to follow you all the way to the doctor's appointment for Popcorn Lung

Pro: You can vape so easily and secretly at work! Just wear a hoodie and you can blow the vape smoke into one of the arm holes after taking a blinker!

Con: Turns out smoke can still get out of your sweater and up into the fire alarm.

Pro: Vaping IS a group activity and if you share it with someone you like it's like you kissed. SOMETHING YOU'LL NEVER DO, WINOS! 5PM PARKING LOT!

Con: Vaping will almost always lead you to getting into a Sharks vs Jets-ian knife fight with the drinkers of the office. Full contact. No cops.

"My Life Is Terrible And I Wish I Was Dead."- An Essay by David, Customer Service.

Hey man! How has it been going? Been settling in nice? I don't know if we met before, but my name is David and I'm a tier 3 worker over in customer service.

How's that department?

Well, let me just put it to you this way: My life is terrible, and I wish I was dead.

Yeah, haha, so it's like - kinda gnarly! But what do you do?

Oh, you were asking about me?

I'm so sorry dude I'm just kinda pre-programmed to respond to other people and ask them how they're doing that sometimes I have a hard time answering questions!

Yeah, my doctor says that it's a not harmful but also hot helpful way that my mind dissociates and allows me to take all of the psychic trauma I get on a day-to-day basis dealing with these customers.

It's awful. These people are terrible. I make practically no money! This job is a literal poverty trap! I'd kill myself but my funeral would cost more than I currently have in the bank so my mom would go in debt!

Why am I trapped in this hell!

But I don't know that's just how I'm feeling, how are you? Do you need help with anything?

You know I may only be tier 3, but I still have access to a variety of our customer service databases so if you need me to look anything up for you I definitely can!

Hold on man one second, I'm actually getting a call. Can I take this?

Hello this is David with smartHaven may I please have your reference number?

Oh, it would be on your email.

You don't know how to do that?

I'm sorry I wasn't trying to yell at you!

I didn't mean to raise my voice, I promise you!

Please I'll break the policy and fully refund this for you.

Just give me a 5 when you get your customer satisfaction form in your email!

They hung up. They always hang up.

I had a dream once. That I bought a lighthouse out in the country but then I realized that I still needed money, so I had to start working. Eventually I forgot all about the lighthouse and was just working constantly to pay my bills and to pay for the lighthouse. It was on autopay, you see. And I woke up in the dream, but I was in another dream, and then I woke up for real.

Why couldn't I have just stayed in that first dream forever?

I try not to think about it. When I do I get angry. I think about how there is no lighthouse except the one you build, and I'll never have a chance to, now that I've given the best and most healthy years of my life to a soulless corporation for nothing in return except for bills, stress, and pain.

So anyways, just let me know if you ever need anything from Customer Service! Great meeting you dude! See you at the holiday party!

How-To Guide: Dealing With The 22-Year-Old Receptionist Who Already Makes More Money Than You!

Step One: Make eye contact as soon as you see them to establish dominance. Remember this feeling when you later look at your negative balance bank account!

Step Two: Ask them about their weekend and while they're droning on about how they went to a desert-vibes concert this weekend you can be imagining the beautiful beachside you'll never be able to afford to retire to. But they will!

Step Three: Invest in a stress ball that you can squeeze tight in your pocket when learning that the receptionist has gotten yet another raise after only being here for 15 months when you have been here for 5 years and have never gotten one!

Step Four: Go full Single White Female and fully take over the identity of the receptionist. Now you are them and you are making more money than you!

*C.O.G. Pro Tip: This likely won't work because you could never be as stunning, funny, and cool as they are but hey, if you get fired or put in jail for identity fraud then you won't have to deal with them anymore! *

Step Five: Accept that you will never be the 22-year-old receptionist, that they will always make more money than you, and that this is your life now!

SURPRISE CHALLENGE!

Can you resist the charm of Accounting Mary Beth's 8-year-old daughter looking to sell Girl Scout cookies or will you stick to your diet?

Hiiiiiii!

This is my daughter, Skye, and she's selling Girl Scout Cookies this holiday season!

Isn't that so cute?!

So, she just wanted to say - go on Skye say it like we practiced!

Hi, my name is Skye and I'm selling Thin Mints and other kinds of kinds too and if you help my Troop #3456489 then we get to go to Universal Studios next year as a treat.

And this year we partnered with The Monsanto Corporation, so the cookies are even bigger and taste great!

Each box is only $15, and all the funds go directly to our troop. How many boxes can I put you down for? Please??

YOU CHOOSE:

Resist!

Yay! You stood your ground and stuck to your diet, way to go! Unfortunately, Mary-Beth now hates you and you get the sinking suspicion someone from the Monsanto Corporation keeps following you home from work!

YOU CHOOSE:

Relent!

What can you do! You can try the diet next year and it will be all the more fulfilling because you'll now have even more weight to lose! Mary-Beth loves you and you've started having dreams where you imagine you are a glowing Monsanto Thin Mint box attacking your enemies at night. But is it a dream? It's probably nothing!

Section Three:
Accepting Your New Life As A Cog!

Part I: The Honeymoon Phase

CHAPTER EIGHT: Your Measly Paycheck!

It's so cool that you've now been here for a couple months and are finally accepting that this is your new life now! Oh, you've not accepted it yet? That's okay! You will! Now that you've gotten your first paycheck let's go over how to spend it! And if you're worried about overspending, don't be! You can't afford to! - **C.O.G. #760**

Did You Know That Our Company Offers A Free Subway Pass For Only $100 Out Of Your Paycheck Every Month?! - An Essay by Mary Beth Keaton, Head of Accounting

Hi so nice to finally meet you and welcome to the smartHaven family! One of the biggest perks of joining our lil' crew here is you get a FREE subway pass for only $100 out of your monthly paycheck!

Isn't that SUCH a cool little perk? I mean most people have to go and buy their subway pass like some slug person. But not you. YOU get a monthly card AND a new subway debit card mailed to you EVERY month thanks to the partnership with smartHaven!

Speechless, right? I was too.

Not ONLY do you get a free subway pass but each month you also have the option of putting up to $200 on your subway debit card which you can use to buy subway passes in the future no matter WHERE you are! And it stays with you even if you leave the company.

So, I will go ahead and opt-in to that option for you and then you'll just notice a line item on every paycheck showing minus $125 to include the free subway pass and the processing fee for your subway debit card. You can't start to use the subway debit card until your 9-month mark, but you know all about that as it was in your contract!

Welcome to the smartHaven family and thank you so much for agreeing to buy into this great free perk of a monthly subway card for ONLY $100 out of your paycheck! Now you're riding with us! Oh, also remember the $25 processing fee too!

Pie Chart - Bye, Bye! The Different Bills, Rent, And Drugs That Will Take Up Your Paycheck!

15% - Coffee, Tea, Caffeine, Nos Energy Drinks, Anti-Sleeping Medication.
5% - Fun drugs that help numb the pain like Weed, Mushrooms, Nicotine, Alcohol, Poppers, Stay-Ups, Put-Downs, or Gas Station Dick Pills From The 7/11 on the corner.
5% - Decorations for your tiny little, cramped apartment. More than enough for at least 3 good chairs, a bed frame, and towels.
50% - Rent and bills! Yup it takes up that much and even more!
2% - Processing fee for bills and rent - what is this shit?
3% - Medications and insurance for medications to help with all of your various ailments and cause new ones in the future!
10% - Bills food and medication for your pet dog or cat. Because if anyone is worth it, it's Dusty. Dusty deserves 100% but we live in an imperfect world.
5% - Wardrobe for work. Business suits. Business casual attire. Business home pajamas to prep you for your next day's work wardrobe.
2% - Free subway pass for only $100 out of your monthly paycheck!
1% - Hair and body care. Being beautiful isn't cheap, except right now for you where it kind of is. Also, bath bombs. So many bath bombs.
2% - Donations to various charities to make up for the sinking feeling you have every day you come home that you're contributing to all of this burning.

Graph – What Each Person In The Office Makes Compared To How Hard They Claim To Be Working

CEO: Making 5 million dollars a year plus stock options and bonuses – **Going all the way to the top, breaking the bounds of the chart in a herculean fashion!**

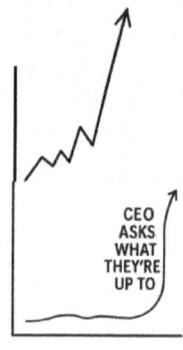

Executive: Making a measly $800,000 a year plus stock options, bonuses, and commissions. **Mostly stays in the middle but then suddenly shoots up to the top when CEO asks what they're up to**

Head of Sales: Making a — frankly depressing — $750,000 a year + 100% of commissions, bonuses, full stock options, and access to secret rich person only island. **SELL! SELL!**

Tom, Customer Service Representative Tier 1: This bougie fat cat makes an incredible $45,000 a year! **Stagnant line at bottom of graph.**

Companion Graph – What Each Person In The Office Makes Compared To How Hard They Actually Work

CEO: **Graph starts out going straight and then makes immediate nosedive.**

Executive: **Chart is flat then moves slightly up when CEO starts asking questions.**

Head of Sales: **No work vacation hog. Line goes negative and breaks the bounds of the graph.**

Tom, Customer Service Representative Tier 1: **Line goes up fast and then goes to straight line - once you've learned how to run on autopilot**

YOU JUST GOT YOUR FIRST PAYCHECK BINGO!

Pay off debts like a boring financially responsible LOSER!	Invest in those stocks your brother's friend keeps yapping about	Slowly move your hand down the check and whisper to yourself, "You're MINE now!"	Go to the casino and see if you can cry your way to getting your money back!	Immediately deposit it into your bank account to avoid the $75 overdraft fee
Treat your most loyal and willing to split it half-sies friend to dinner	Finally show that swindler on main street that you have the money to invest in his instruments!	Get a Costco membership and buy one hundred $1.50 hot dogs to eat for the rest of your natural born life	Invest in drugs, alcohol, or any other vice to distract yourself from how little money you actually made	Treat your significant other to a lovely meal in the hopes that they will forget you still owe their parents $5000
Create new debts that you promise will be paid off next month	Realize that money isn't real, time is an illusion, and you still have to work weekends	**FREE SPACE:** Turns out a lot more than you budgeted for goes straight to taxes!	Call your grandmother to tell her how excited you are to get your first paycheck and then guilt her into sending you letter with a $100 check and 15 newspaper clippings	Go to the casino and put it all on black!
Pay health, car, auto, water, gas, internet, PlayStation+, and OnlyFans monthly premiums	Go to the casino and put it all on red!	Treat your cat to an expensive cat toy only to find out they actually prefer the box instead	Buy some extra tchotchkes to put on your lame desk in the hope that it will get your office crush to talk to you!	Use it to finally see some real, legitimate theater like you always wanted. Wait, this show cost $200?!
Pay for that inhaler you've always been wanting and have medically needed for the last 3 years but couldn't afford	Impress your local 7/11 by finally being able to buy the share sized peanut M&Ms	Help financially support struggling artists on Etsy, TikTok, and your one cousin who does "art"	Eat like a king and then realize the next morning the next 29 days you need to eat like an especially poor peasant	Donate $25 to PBS to finally live up to the promise you made the Arthur cartoon when you were 8-years-old

Challenge:

Can you go an entire week without spending 50% of your paycheck???

Weekly CALENDAR

SUNDAY	MONDAY	TUESDAY	WEDNESDAY	THURSDAY	FRIDAY	SATURDAY
GO TO CHURCH TO CONFESS YOUR SINS?	PAY FOR MEDICINE?	DINNER?	RENT?	NIECE'S 9TH BIRTHDAY PARTY?	GO OUT AND DRINK AWAY THE PAIN?	FIX YOUR CAR?

If you circle any of them instead of marking them with a big X you fail!

CHAPTER NINE: Your Lame Desk!

I love desk! The Desk is where I can show off my creativity and put up FUN pictures that inspire me and make me want to work harder!
Let's get started with something I LOVE - picture frames!
All mine are empty! - **C.O.G. #760**

List: The Best Small Picture Frames You Can Put On Your Desk And Then Gently Move Your Hand Down While Whispering, "Remember, You're Doing It For Them" To!

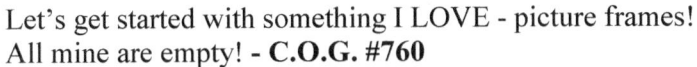

This is the **Rustic Acres Classic Picture Frame.** Great for highlighting a family member or loved one whom you're doing all this for. And don't you forget that.

The **Ikea Standard Frame**. This slightly bigger frame allows for a more intimate experience when thinking about your loved ones and how they're all that's keeping you bound to this mortal plane we call sanity.

The **Double Picture Frame**. Now you can put two loved ones next to each other or mix and match! Both frames are just the right size for a single hand so you should have no problem if you want to double palm both frames after a swift moment of realization.

Photo Cube: Do not recommend very painful on your hands and have sharp edges. Avoid!

The Sustani Cube-Desk Frame: Like the photo cube but good! And even better it has a box built in so you can put work items in there and maximize your day!

POV: Your Lame Desk

Cube wall: Great for deeply sighing and lightly resting your head on! Not great for hitting because they are paper thin and you will hit Meredith one cubicle over

Picture of your loved ones you can shamefully turn down on their face when forced by your boss to do something ethically questionable

Computer: Only the latest 2006 Pentium Processors exclusively running a computer system 10 years older than it

Clock: Only 15 more minutes until you're free (for the next 8 hours)

Phone: The loudest fucking phone you have ever heard in your goddamn life

Desktop: Where you can put various Funko Pops or any kind of highly delicate figurine because who are you kidding, this is who you are

Under desk: Plenty of space for pet, child, or situationship to hide

Desk: Where you hide your therapy bunny Hoppenheimer

Chair: The standard in uncomfort with 3 adjustable levels!

List: Dolls and Other Tchotchkes You Can Put On Your Desk Ranked Upon How Judgmental Your Co-Workers Would Be Of Them

3 Little Ornate Glass Mushroom Headed Men: They do look kind of scary up close and seem very fragile but I guess they're okay?

Funko Pop: As long as it's not a weird custom one like Roman Polanski, Timothy McVeigh, or Cee-Lo Green and isn't still in the box, almost everyone will think it's okay! A little judged though I mean you are an adult, David.

Tiny Little Smiling Porcelain Children: Honestly, they make me very uncomfortable with their little eyes so they're way worse than a Funko Pop.

Doll/Action Figure: I mean it depends on the figure, but this is not ideal. You are now actively being judged more than agreed with. I thought we went over this, David, but you still keep doing this and now we're gonna have to put you in the box.

Warhammer/Lego/Any Kind Of Overly Involved Set Up: Who are you trying to impress here? It's certainly not us. I mean, good for having a hobby, but this is too much. David, don't end up like this, promise!

Percentages Of Your Desk

15% Various papers with either important information or pointless scribble

25% The enormous computer they gave you that is at least 15 years old

10% Sticky notes containing positive mantras, helpful notes, and all-caps curses

10% Tape that you have been hoarding just to feel a little thrill

5% Picture of your loved ones looking at you all judgmental and loving

1% Your car and apartment keys which you've somehow lost- oh no!!

5% Leftover boxes used to transport pieces of desk to potential new desk

3% Pungent candle that Shaun in Fulfillment insists will "mellow you out"

2% Chords and chargers tangled together like a group of rats in the sewer

4% Office supplies that you are hoarding and secretly take home with you at night

7% Assorted company memorabilia given to during the holidays in lieu of a raise

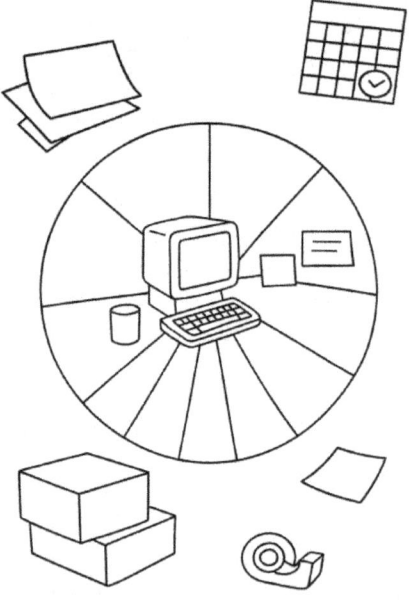

3% Unfinished coffees that are probably still okay to drink if you really need to

5% Tissues, paper towels, wet wipes, screen cleaners, air cannons, Febreze Spray

5% Calendar that has dates circled in red as if you weren't under enough stress

Rating The Desks In The Office

Sharon, Finance: 9/10 - This refined desk boasts 4 different pictures of Sharon's large Cape Cod summer-ing family and is spotless every day because Sharon clearly has some sort of psychological thing about cleanliness.

David, Customer Support: 6/10 - Way too many little figurines and way too many opened and not finished boxes of cereal.

Chris, CEO: 10/10 - When you have a cleaning staff dedicated just to your desk and the money to buy whatever you want your desk is going to look amazing, if soulless. But don't you dare tell him I said that!

Shaun, Fulfillment: 7/10 - Pretty messy you think but also impossible to find again and shrouded in mystery, much like Shaun.

Diane, Accounting: 5/10 - At first glance this desk looks like a 10/10 but the closer you get you realize everything beautiful on her desk is related to her multi-level-marketing schemes she keeps trying to rope you into.

Your Supervisor: 8/10 - Somehow super clean and well put together despite them being "too busy to chat" anytime you need something.

Becca, 22-year-old Receptionist: 1/10 - Her desk is empty because "potential clients prefer to see it that way when they check in" or some bullshit.

Your Desk: 8.5/10 - Even better than your supervisor's desk in terms of neatness, not that anyone cares!

"Look There's Nothing Wrong With Me, I Just Like Having Cereal Close To Me At All Times" - An Essay By Office Semi-Creep Martin In Tech Support!

Oh..sorry..let me just get behind you...

Hey.

It's me. Martin. From tech support. I know you are seeing everyone's desks now, but I just wanted to tell you I just like having cereal close to me, and on my desk. Other than that, there is NOTHING wrong with me!

You're a new employee so I just wanted to set the record straight. A lot of people just look at me and write me off as if I'm some kind of creep, but I'm not. I just move in silence and love cereal!

I'm 6 foot 9. I exclusively wear black clothing and have trained in karate. That's why I'm so lanky and fast. I'm NOT weird and nothing about my desk is weird!

When I was a child, mother would always make me cereal.

Now that her spirit is in me, and she is gone I must praise her by eating cereal exclusively at my desk and never in the office kitchen.

Also, I have a lot of work to do, everyone here is terrible with technology, and no one listens to my advice, which I often whisper so they may hear it better.

Anyways I just wanted to tell you that, so you knew that I may be weird but I'm not weird BECAUSE of the eating of the cereal.

Also, you have a bunch of viruses on your computer. What kind of weird stuff have you been clicking on!

CHAPTER TEN: Day-To-Day Office Life!

Oh my god!! Don't you just LOVE that you're a full part of the team now? Now you get to experience all the fun eccentricities of the office all while doing whatever it is your job is! Let's start at where's most important - THE OFFICE KITCHEN FRIDGE! - **C.O.G. #760**

Inside The Company Fridge!

Bottom Row: Office lunches that have different names on them but are all free game if you make more than the person whose name is on it.

Middle Row: Free Drink Land - this is where the free drinks provided by the office will reside for the 15 minutes they are available every quarter before the workers descend on it and take what's been placed out.

Top Row: CEO Bait Lunch - Not the actual CEO's lunch - he gets that delivered - this is merely a test to see who steals this as there is a tracker inside it. Depending on how they stole it they will either be promoted or fired.

Side Bottom: Various assortment of crusted up condiments that you shouldn't use if you value your health.

Side Top: Completely empty to remind you that you are ultimately nothing. Please note the fridge in the Executive Suites has this section filled with Rosé. You'd like that, wouldn't you, you little cretin!

Freezer: Packed to the brim with frozen lunches and dinners to be consumed by the Customer Service team during their 15 minute breaks between talking

List: The Best Free Drinks Available In The Office Kitchen Fridge Ranked!

1. Red Bull Xtra Xtra Sugar
2. Energy Water
3. Carbonated Water
4. Soda That's Not Pepsi
5. "Fruit" Juice
6. Mason Jar Filled With Green Liquid
7. Pepsi
8. Off-Off Brand La Croix Called Le Crex
9. Energy Drink That Expired In 2004 But Looks Safe-ish
10. Plant-Based Gloop That Tastes Surprisingly Good
11. Kool-Aid But Only The Bad Flavors
12. 1978 Spanish Dessert Wine That's Somehow Here
13. Sugar Free Pepsi
14. Plain Water In A Coffee Cup
15. Pepsi MAX

Different Coffee Brands You'll Use To Wake You Up So You Can Live Another Day In Service Of The Almighty Dollar!

Super-Secret Guide On How To Escape At 4pm Instead Of 5pm On Fridays.

Step One: Buy a high quality Army ghillie suit online and wear it to work all day until 3:59pm.

Step Two: Disguised, pull the fire alarm at exactly 4pm and use your grappling hook to quickly get to the ceiling.

Step Three: While hidden in the ventilation system set up a little bed so you can hide from your co-workers once they come back inside.

Step Four: Realize, "Wait, I was trying to escape from work. Why does this plan involve me hiding in the work vents until Monday?!" Contemplate the decisions you have made, shimmy down from the vents to your chair and attempt to leave the building only to realize you pulling the fire alarm in step 2 has caused the door to be locked.

Step Five: Accept that you should've just said you were feeling sick at 3:45pm on Friday instead of buying a non-refundable ghillie suit, grappling hook, and sleeping bag and wasting your weekend locked at work. Maybe next Friday!

Pro/Con: The Printer/Copier: Friend or Foe?

Pro: It prints everything you can't at home because you can't afford one right now!

Con: All the pages slightly bleed ink because this printer is 87 years old and in printer terms is "dying a slow, inky death."

Pro: Has so many different options! You want to print? You want to copy? You want to collate?

Con: Per your employee contract each additional option after print does cost you .25 hours of off time.

Pro: Is constantly breaking down so it provides a great, natural excuse for you to not be doing work.

Con: Constantly break down in the middle of printing, copying, and especially collating.

Pro: Has no memory feature so you can use it to print out copies of your resume if you decide to use your lunch break to interview for other jobs.

Con: Does have a snitch feature and unless you do an ink check will tell your supervisor you've been printing resumes.

Pro: Never broke down on you when you were going through that break up with your co-worker, Becca.

Con: Is this reason your co-worker, Becca, broke up with you!

"For The Love Of God Please Stop Eating My Lunches Or I Will Enact My Righteous Fury On All Of You." - An Essay By Andrew, The Guy In The Cubicle Next To You Who Keeps Getting His Lunches Stolen

Hey man! It's me, Andrew!

We work in the same department, I'm in the cubicle next to you! Oh yeah, now you remember me.

Wait, don't turn around!

Look, do you know who has been eating my lunches? I have worked here for over five years and like clockwork at least one day per week one of my lunches is stolen from the fridge. Do you know who is doing this? I promise I won't be mad at you.

I do, however, promise that if this continues this office and its inhabitants shall know a righteous fury unlike anything they have ever experienced before. I will be repaid what was taken from me and then I will pay back in full what is owed. One co-worker per sandwich that has been taken until the thief comes forward. Justice.

Wait, don't turn back around and please don't tell anyone I said that!

I was just kidding and I realized towards the end there it was becoming a little shooter-y. I'm just really upset is all. I put so much care into making those lunches that for someone to steal them and for it to happen once every week for 5 years straight it just breaks my heart.

I know that you would never do so please know that any righteous, non-violent at first, fury will never be directed at you because I know that you're an honest person. I know you would tell me if you knew who was eating them.

I know that if it were you in fact who were eating my sandwiches you would need to proceed very carefully. Whoever has eaten my lunches is due their punishment by my righteous fury. I will be an instrument of lunchtime revenge. And if you were the one who played me, this instrument will BIND you with its strings!

Wait wait wait please don't get up! You've noticed it all these years too, right?!

You've only worked here for 6 months now, so it couldn't possibly be you and you haven't noticed anything because you buy lunch out every day?

Oh my god I am so sorry! I can't believe I just blew up on you like that and you haven't even been here for that long!

Rage really did blind me. Just let me know if you ever do see anything, okay?

Those will be the deceivers and thieves I will enact my righteous fury on.

Which again, I just want to stress, is NOT anything related to violence!

Unless they push me too far.

Part II: Further Into The Heart of Darkness, Marlow

CHAPTER ELEVEN: Performance Reviews!

OH MY GOD! Are you nervous?! Performance reviews can be really scary! If I were to do bad and lose my job, who would I be then? I don't like to think about that, so I follow these tips instead! Let's start with some wisdom from a GOOD **Karen**, your team leader! - **C.O.G. #760**

"Look I Know That I Only See You Once Every 2 Weeks For About 15-20 Uncomfortable Minutes, But I Think I Know Enough To Judge You On! - An Essay By Your Team Leader Karen

Hey bud go ahead and close the door behind you!

So, your quarterly performance review is coming up right now and I just wanted to check in with you and also kind of assuage some fears you might have, does that sound good? Okay, great!

So, listen, bud - I know you might be worried about this review because we really only talk every 2 weeks at our 10-15 minute 1:1 meetings, but I just want you to know that I'm confident I've gained enough from those to fully judge you!

So don't you worry because you are in good hands!

So, tell me again when did you start here? Oh, about six months ago? OHHH right. Haha - this is your quarterly review! Oh man I kinda forgot it for a second.

So, I looked at your scores for the past six months, I promise for real, and they looked good. You are definitely getting the hang of this! That said I do see some room where we can make some improvements.

So, let's start by you telling me what it is you do during the day from when you get here to when you leave and how you think that has gone? Great. That's exactly what I thought you were going to say and what you did. Keep up the good work!

So, bud. I think we can agree on one thing: You're doing your job and with some minor improvements you can do it even better. But great job so far and I am now definitely fully understanding what it is you do here which is also great. Okay, bud, that's our time. Can you tell Kevin to come in next! Wait, that's you? Then who's Kevin?

 # List: Items In Your Supervisor's Office You Can Look Out While They Search For Information They Should've Had Already Prepared!

1. Picture of partner who is somehow super-hot.
2. Little bobblehead of supervisor made to commemorate Q3.
3. A drawer that is just covered in Post-It-Notes that say things like, "Password is 6789" and "DON'T FORGET TO TAKE INSULIN!"
4. Lil' notepad filled with doodles and plot for the self-published fantasy novel Baldus's Requiem they are currently working on off the clock.
5. Life-size poster of The Rock thanking your supervisor for selling his tequila on the side.
6. Character sketches for their self-published fantasy novel Baldus's Requiem.
7. Award from 20 years ago that they will talk about for 15 minutes.
8. Video camera suspiciously pointed directly at you with boom mic.
9. Headshots from when your supervisor tried acting under the stage name Sean Richard Danger.
10. Pictures of their family and mean dog.
11. Their application to film school.
12. An ironing board.
13. Their pet for some reason?
14. Large cereal box filled with mix of Reece's, Lucky Charms, and Pumpkin Spice Cheerios.
15. 3 different half-finished Subway sandwiches formed into one mega-sandwich.

List: Names You Will Be Called By Your Supervisor Instead Of Your Actual Name

1. Champ
2. Buddy
3. Old Buddy, My Champ!
4. "Remind Me Your Name Again?"
5. My Favorite [Your Job Title]!
6. David?
7. My Main Man!
8. My Fly Girl!
9. My Favorite Non-Gendered Worker!
10. Le Bon Travailleur
11. The Person Becca Keeps Saying Is Flirtatiously Starring At
12. My Good Friend Who Needs No Introduction
13. Dr. Phone Call
14. The Bain Of My Existence!
15. The Light Of My Life!
16. You're Sure It's Not David? Because I Know We've Got A Few Davids
17. Old Smelly Gym Bag Themselves
18. My Confidant
19. Formerly Known By HR As Do Not Hire
20. CEO's Nephew

Anatomy of A Supervisor/Team Leader/Whatever Dumb Name They're Making You Call Them Like Support Sensei Or Head Of Talk

EYES: Focused on something that's a little bit more important than whatever you're trying to ask right now!

MOUTH: Used to spew company approved propaganda/quotas/fun run locations

ARMS: Either dangly lil' noodle arms or way too buff in a concerning way

HEART: Either cold and gone or too big and a liability for a job where you have to fire people

STOMACH: Surely fucked up from years of Subway sandwiches eaten and they do get a lunch break

HIPS/BUTT: Trust me, you want no part in this. Turn around.

HANDS: Calloused and tired from working so hard. Just kidding!

How-To Guide: How To Walk Dramatically Out Of A Bad Performance Review In Order To Gain Sympathy From Co-Workers.

Step One: Take a deep breath and prepare yourself. You are about to put on the greatest acting performance of your life

Step Two: Open your supervisor's door quietly, look around wistfully, and return back to your desk.

Step Three: Stand up from your desk, let out a deep sigh, and begin walking back over to supervisor's door.

Step Four: Reach for the door handle, turn to your co-workers, and say, "No! I just can't put myself through that again!"

Step Five: Start a slow clap and say, "I'm doing this for ME!" and walk back to your desk triumphantly as your co-workers cheer for you.

Percentages Of Your Performance Review

1%: Shockingly helpful feedback that will make you better at your job

2%: Wondering if this meeting being so long is a good thing or a bad thing?

3%: Trying to make this meeting extra-long with drawn out, pointless questions once you realize you can't go back to work until you're finished

4%: Yapping in the hopes of getting some kind of raise only to be told moments later this is not a meeting where raises can be discussed

5%: Looking out the window and letting your intrusive thoughts take over for one brief, glorious moment!

5%: Actual numbers of how you are doing confusing named something overlong like Key Performance Indication or Total Work Indicator

10%: Asking you to "hold on really quick for a second" so that your supervisor can get together the papers on you they've had an entire month to get ready

10%: Asking you for feedback on how they are doing because this is actually their performance review too somehow?

15%: Asking your supervisor how their fiancée, pet, and/or family are doing only to receive a long, weepy story about how things are "not going well"

25%: Trying to pry personal information from you about your dating life or lack thereof in the hopes of making themselves feel better about their life

20%: Wondering how in the world your supervisor can afford all of this stuff when they only make $3000 per year more than you. Is it a family money thing?

CHAPTER TWELVE: Birthdays In The Office: Hey At Least You Get Cake!

Happy Birthday! Happy Birthday! It's someone in the office's birthday! What a fun little treat for all of us! We're all passing around a card for Janet so could you please sign it?! Not sure what to write? Okay, let's start there! - **C.O.G. #760**

List: Hope It's A Great Day! And Other Hollow Statements You Can Sign On A Birthday Card Before Passing It Onto Another Poor Soul!

1. Best of luck with your birthday!
2. You, (NAME), really help make this office shine!
3. Hope you get EVERYTHING you wished for!
4. Birthdays are what make life worth living! Nothing else.
5. It's always so nice seeing you only in the office!
6. It's that day again! The day we all feared! Just kidding!
7. I hope the day you were born is as fun as today is!
8. Get it birthday king/queen!
9. I've never written in cursive before! Am I doing it right?
10. Happy Birthday me love you!
11. I've seen your birthday next year already so get ready for a great year!
12. If you can make it to another birthday, so can I!
13. My present for you will be delivered in secret and via crow!
14. We've never met before, but I wish you the best unless you're B2B!
15. Where is my cake! Really though!
16. Just remember you need to work extra for the minutes I used to write this!
17. Remember that night on Paradise Island? I still do.
18. Excuse me, what year is it?
19. Birthday! That's it!
20. Hope it's a great day!

Interactive Card Signing Challenge: Can You Sign A Birthday Card For Angela? She Has No Clue Who You Are, But I Guess You Still Have To Sign This?

"Happy Birthday Angela! Hope your eyesight is almost fully back to 100%!" - Dave (Marketing)

"Happy Birthday Angela! Save a piece of cake for me! JK I already cut out a piece for myself! - Sean (CFO)

"Angela! Best of luck with your birthday! - David(?) (Customer Service)

"Angela! I knew it was your birthday because I know everyone's birthday! Hope you have fun tonight at 8pm at the Crocodile Bar on 5th and Hopper St in the seat near the window!" - Susan (HR)

"Angela, I send you all of my love! Happy Birthday, Happy Year, Happy to work with you!" - No name

How-To Guide: Making Strategic Alliances And Friendships With People You Will Hopefully Never Have To Interact With Outside Of Work!

Step One: Scan the room, look for anyone paying attention, and anyone seated near the exits. These are the high value targets.

Step Two: Get the social media info of those people and stalk them to learn all of their interests. Select the co-workers that have interests you'd be okay hearing about regularly, but also okay with never actually doing outside of work.

Step Three: Casually bring up one of their interests at the weekly Friday Happy Hour. Allow them to continue talking about it by simply responding, "Hmmm" or "That is SO interesting" to anything they say and pivot the conversation back to them when they ask you what your interests are!

★C.O.G. Pro Tip: Thankfully the Customer Service workers aren't allowed to have breaks, so you don't have to worry about dealing with them! ★

Step Four: At the end of the night after you're friends take four different ways home to make sure you aren't being tailed. They can NEVER know where you live!

Step Five: Create a spreadsheet with all of the information on your new friends. Print it out and laminate it so that you can covertly look at it whenever you need a refresher on what their names are, what things they like, and how that can help you!

~~Pie~~ Cake Chart: Percentages Of Different Kind Of Birthday Cakes You Will Get

1%: A $500 Three-Tiered Artisan Cake Available Only To CEO
3%: Cake That Actually Has Your Name Spelt Correctly On It
4%: THC Infused Cake Because They Let Shaun In Fulfillment Bake It
5%: An Empty Plate Of Crumbs Because Someone Ate All Of It Secretly
10%: Confetti Cake Because Diane Knows You're Going Through A Rough Patch
15%: Cake That Has Your Name Spelt Wrong And Just Says "Goo Job"
22%: Horrific Frankenstein Cake Made Of Ingredients In Company Kitchen
40%: The Cheapest Option Available - Vanilla With Vanilla Frosting

"I Know I Make Millions Of Dollars Per Year But You Have To Understand It's Been Rough For Me So I Can't Really Afford More Than A $5 Amazon Gift Card Right Now" - An Essay by the CEO, Charles Welde the III

Yeah..Yeah no that's exactly what I told him too.

Hey sorry I'll call you later - Oh hey there!

You came to collect Angela's gift, right? Thank you so much for coming and honestly now that you're here I just wanted to make sure you and Angela understood why the gift card was only for $5.

Look, this year has been SO tough on everyone, especially me. I really came to realize this year what's important to me. And my millions of dollars from my family and this job aren't what's important. My work isn't what's important. I AM IMPORTANT.

Wow. That felt pretty big to say out loud! Obviously, you'll never repeat this to anyone, but man that felt GOOD.

It's like I LOVE Angela, whomever she may be and whatever department she may work in, just like how I love ALL of my people but I also at the end of the day need to think about me. Self-Care.

That's why I could only give her and everyone else this year a $5 gift card to Amazon.com. I spent all the rest of my gift money on an even more important gift: the gift of therapy to me from myself!

Angela won't get to have the chance to have another year here and get another $5 card if ME, the CEO, isn't fully aligned. It's just how business works these days. That's what my therapist said at least. I'm paying him with what I could pay you guys so that I can pay myself again in the future and then we'll ALL get paid. It's simple!

I FINALLY have clarity. Isn't that so great? Even better therapy only cost a few million dollars, which is like 3 months for me, so I was totally fine.

Ok I have to get back on that call so here's the card for Angela and I'll see you later. Close the door on your way out please. Thanks!

CHAPTER THIRTEEN: Meetings!

Yay! One of my FAVORITE parts of working, besides
helping make smartHaven a better place at the expense of
myself, is to go to MEETINGS! I love them so much I try to
make them go as long as possible! Here's some of my tips
for you for them, you're going to LOVE these! Please tell me
you love them! - **C.O.G. #760**

List: Different Ways To Draw Out Meetings So That You Don't Have To Go Back To Work

1. Simply ask "Why?" and then when someone asks you what you mean just say, "Well, I didn't really understand the last slide and I think a lot of people have questions about it." Ding, Ding, Ding you just added on at least 5-10 more minutes!
2. Say aloud, "I just heard from the Brisbane Office, they don't like this one bit, we've got to go back to the drawing board. What should I tell them?" and wait while a general confusion and anxiety comes over your co-workers. Do we have a Brisbane office? Where is Brisbane? Are people getting to go to Brisbane and not telling me? If you act well enough this can add a nice 15-20 minutes to your meeting!
3. Ask if you can test out the fire alarm to see just how loud that baby can get!
4. Convince the douchiest person in the office to challenge one of your female co-workers into spraying him with their mace because "he can take it!" He cannot and this will buy you 30 minutes to even an hour!
5. Tell everyone that you wrote a Hamlet-Ian play-within-a-play about the workplace and you need time to prepare and perform it for them now. Improvise a 4-hour play with full tech, props, and costumes. No pressure!
6. Ask everyone in the room to please remind them of their first, middle, and last names!
7. Bring in a beach ball and tell everyone they can't leave until we achieve "beach vibes."
8. Tell everyone you have a video presentation but it's actually just all three extended editions of The Lord of The Rings edited together into one movie.
9. Say that you heard the Brisbane office does their meetings even longer and that they said we're wimps for not going longer.
10. Go to the bathroom as soon as the meeting starts and don't come out for 90 minutes.

How-To Guide: How To Tell If This Is Going To Be A Boring Meeting Or A Now-I-Am-Scared-I-Might-Get-Laid-Off Kind Of Meeting!

Tip #1: Look at management's eyes – are they the normal glazed-over-because-they-hate-meetings eyes or are they the I-need-to-look-down-or-they'll-know eyes? If it's the latter, you're done!

Tip #2: How many chairs are set up? A few, that's fine! A lot though, could mean the entire management team is speaking in which case you might need to revive that LinkedIn account!

Tip #3: Is HR nowhere to be seen or sitting in the corner looking down nervously at their phone? Nowhere to be seen? You're a-ok! Looking down at phone? Uh oh.

Tip #4: Does it seem like there are more security guards working today than usual and all of them have stopwatches? If so, it's not looking good!

Tip #5: Did they let you leave after the meeting ended or did they just lay you off right there? If so, watch out this might mean you are being laid off!

List: Non-Sequester Questions You Can Ask In A Meeting To Really Make It Go Off The Rails

1. "That's very interesting what you said about this quarter, did you know that they're going to start phasing out the penny soon? Copper is too expensive. Can you believe that?"
2. "Where did the Caesar dressing in the refrigerator go? If you tell me now, I won't be mad."
3. "While we're all here, Lauren, why don't you tell everyone what you told me about Mary Kay?"
4. "Where exactly IS fulfillment located?"
5. "Marry, Fuck, Kill: Chick-fil-A, Popeyes, Raising Canes?"
6. "Did you know that on your birthday you can go to any Costco, and they have to give you a full tank of gas?"
7. "If there was a fire right now, who would you save and who would you let burn and why?"
8. "Does time even exist?"
9. "If you had to give a first and last name to every letter in the alphabet, what would they be?"
10. "Do you think birds know that I hate them?"

MEETING THAT COULD'VE BEEN AN EMAIL BINGO!

Someone said screw it and brought their dog into the meeting	"I know we all want to get back to work so I'll be quick" says liar	Mark from Sales makes what he thinks is a pretty good point but is actually just what Sharon said, but louder	Company wino Daryl is taking secret swigs of his favorite Malbec while no is looking	Oh great, the CEO has decided he wants to sit in on this meeting!
Incessant yammering about a topic no one cares about but no one has the guts to say for fear of reprisal	No one is prepared yet somehow everyone was on time and wants to leave early	Someone who brought their cat to the meeting really questioning their choices	Promise of sandwiches for meeting instantly reneged on	Actual good points are made and ideas are raised but we're already 5 minutes over so who cares?
Weirdo who brings his pet toad with them to every meeting acting like this is totally normal	You discover a hidden talent for art as you doodle an unflattering portrait of whoever is yapping right now	**FREE SPACE: Meeting has to be at 5:30 PM to accommodate smartHaven's New Caledonian counterpart co-workers!**	Company vaper also tries his luck and the proceeding cloud sets off the fire alarm and fire sprinklers	"I feel like this could've just been an email" says the bravest soul you will ever meet who will be reprimanded following this meeting
You enter the meeting not knowing anything and somehow leave it knowing less than you did before	Everyone's faces fill with rage as someone who wasn't paying attention asks a question that was answered 28 minutes ago	Becca the 22-year-old receptionist can't get the projector to work even though that's one of only 5 total tasks she has for her job	"Hey, can we please focus back on the meeting?" says company brown-noser and snitch	Gen Z co-worker Zander continues thumbing through his own loud TikTok's
David from Customer Service keeps nervously looking at his watch because he knows he will be penalized if he is not back in exactly 30 minutes	75% of meeting filled recapping last meeting	Projector finally starts working and then immediately shuts down again when someone try to adjust the volume	Sharon from Finance actually makes a pretty going point making you rethink this meeting was completely pointless	Words "Agenda,""Support," and "Service" are written on the white board like hieroglyphics

"Eat Me. Do It. Put Me In Your Dirty Little Bellies. I Accept My Fate." A Defiant Essay/Last Will And Testament By The 20 Inch Party Sub Bought Specifically For This Meeting

What are you looking at, broski? You're asking yourself: How am I talking to you right now without any mouth? The answer is simple: psychic connection.

I've lived a long and happy life of 20 years. I fought in the Chipotle Sauce Wars of 2015. Hell, I ate other sandwiches during the Long Restock of 2020!

Oh, don't look at me like that! You're gonna eat me as soon as Diane stops blabbing but I'm the bad guy for having eaten a few fellow party subs when I was hungry?

That's what I thought. Show me some respect in these last moments, please.

Part of me wants you to eat me. To stick me good in your bellies and to feel the stomach acid as it burns me.

Would that still be enough punishment for my sins?

I had a son once. He was a footlong meatball. Pure Italian stallion.
I wasn't watching him one day and somebody ordered him. I couldn't believe it. I mean no one eats meatballs, and why my meatball sandwich? My wife left me soon after. She said I made our heating tray bed feel like a jail cell and that she wanted to be with her son.

She threw herself into the trash later that night. They took it out at the start of the morning shift, so I never even got a chance to say goodbye to her either.

I knew I had to try and absolve my sins. The only problem was I didn't see 'em as sins. I still don't. I see them both as very unfortunate accidents. The kind that happens in the life of a 20 inch party sub.

Ain't nobody's fault. We all get to the end of the line sometime. Guess I've finally gotten to mine. And I'm telling you now, I'm not going out without a fight.

We're friends now so I'll tell you but the left side of me is completely rotten by now. I don't know if that could really harm someone any more than just making them sick, but I hope it does make them sick.

Why?

Because fuck you humans, that's why!

Why do you get to live full lives with families and pleasure but we, the sandwiches are stuck baking in the oven and going down your filthy little gullets you call mouths. I was created by humans with the sole purpose of being eaten. I was made to be served.

Why?

What did I do to deserve this punishment and why was I given the gift of feeling? Are you god? Do you even know?

Can a 20 inch party sub really in good faith feed a room of 25 different people? I mean who was in charge of that decision? You couldn't've at least gotten a bigger sub or maybe one or two more of me? At least give me someone to talk to?

Was it Diane? God, I fucking knew it.

Why?

Because this has Diane written all over it. I've only been in this meeting for 50 minutes and I can already tell you everything that is wrong with Diane.

Ya know what? Do me a favor?

Have her eat the left side. I lived a life with remembering and I regret nothing!

Sic Semper Tyrannis!

CHAPTER FOURTEEN: The Various Sad And Half-Hearted Attempts Your Company Will Make To Have You Feel Like A Family Member!

Hey Bud! Remember when I said we were like a family? Well, here's all the ways we are! I already heard your section got picked to be this month's cleaning team The Tidys! Don't be nervous though because I have some great advice for you! Let's first get a list of all the FUN things the company will do! - **C.O.G. #760**

List: The Various Sad And Half-Hearted Attempts Your Company Will Make To Have You Feel Like Part Of The Team!

1. **Bar Night!** – It will scare you how some people are exactly the same when drunk!
2. **Company Game Days!** – We're devoting the whole day to company bonding unless you work in a department that affects our daily revenue in which case you will not be joining!
3. **Company Partially Funded Tech Classes!** - Learn how to code with Martin who has never spoken to a woman this long without him getting in trouble!
4. **Company Concert At Company Mandated 5-Day Development Seminar!** - We got two out of the three members of Third Eye Blind to sing you guys off the ledge! Isn't that cool!
5. **Company Blood Drive!** - The CEO is donating too! Isn't he so cool?!
6. **Company Squid Game!** - The entire company watches the first season of Squid Game in an effort to foster a friendly work environment!
7. **Company One-Act-Play Night!** - Everyone is writing their best plays and presenting them on a Saturday unless you have work then, then you won't!
8. **Company Bar Crawl!** - This will be remembered as a TERRIBLE idea!
9. **Company Spades And Uno Tournament!** - Somehow ends worse than the bar crawl!
10. **Company Blood Re-Draw!** - Turns out the CEO forgot he's actually O+ not B- so he wants to just do this again because he admits his mistakes!
11. **Company Skeet Shooting Competition!** - And the guns are being handled by the shiftiest person in the office, Blake!
12. **Company Show Us Your Family Day!** - Just to make sure you have one!
13. **Company Dirt Bike Motocross Extravaganza!** - Okay, this one is pretty cool!
14. **Company Blood Re-Re-Draw**! We promise this is the last one!

15. **Company Kidz Day!** - We let all the children run the company! It's terrible!

Texts From Your Boss Telling You To Come To The Totally Not Required Company 5K Fun Run!

 Text 7:35 AM: Hey bud! Just checking to see are you coming to the 5K today? ;)

Text 7:45 AM: Good morning! Hope you have your shoes on the company 5K starts in 45 minutes!

Text 8:00 AM: 30 Minutes now! :0

Text 8:05 AM: Hey man I know this isn't required but we hope to see you! Everyone else is here and they all say they miss you!

Text 8:15 AM: Hey, we need a headcount of everyone doing the 5K are you coming or not? Really disappointed you haven't responded yet. Very unlike you.

Text 8:30 AM: We'll see you at the finish line! I hope ;) Seriously though, you should be there.

Text 10 AM: WELL, THE RACE IS OVER NOW! WHERE THE HELL WERE YOU? I know I said it wasn't required to come but literally everyone important was there. We're definitely going to need to talk on Monday about this. I'm really hurt and so are others!

Text 11 AM: OMG!!!!! Just saw on the news that you were on that train that derailed! Ignore all my other messages lol! Are you okay? Can you walk? This might be crazy, but they do have another 5K today and you're already full of adrenaline from saving all those people! Call me!

"This Was My Fault And I'm Taking Responsibility For This And From You, Who I Also See As Responsible For This, And Who Will Be Punished" An Apologetic Essay by the CEO, Charles Welde the III He's Only Giving Because An Expose On Him Was Just Published

We messed up.

There I said it. Feels kind of good to address the elephant in the room. I would like to formally apologize for all of the allegations that were printed in *Rolling Stone* about me and my "radioactive-level toxic workplace"

These people attacked me and worst of all, they attacked you. And I won't stand for it!

That is why I, and I alone have decided to take the blame for the toxic environment that we all had a hand in creating. I am the CEO so I will take the blame. That's what good leaders do.

But just because I'm the martyr here doesn't mean that there won't be some difficult days in the day to come.

We're going to have to make *Rolling Stone* think that we've made meaningful changes and that means that some of you who, in my opinion, are the real toxic workplace facilitators, will have their positions terminated.

Their losses are really going to hurt me and all of us and I personally will take them as a lesson going forward.

And speaking of going forward, going forward we will be instituting a no cell phone policy.

Obviously this story came as a result of leaks to *Rolling Stone* so to protect all of us from having all of our misdeeds released we will be collecting everyone's phones every morning and placing them in dampening pouches until you leave.

I'm really sorry that this has happened and really disappointed in you all for letting it get this far. Did I throw a stapler or two? Yes. Did you not say anything afterwards, making me think this was okay? Yes. So you see you enabled me with your silence, which is really problematic.

Now because of your silence and implicit approval I felt emboldened to do other things like date multiple assistants at once, use my office for weekend parties that I made you work as unpaid staff, and even more I can't remember because you also emboldened me to try cocaine, which I am now addicted to!

Take a deep breath. In. Out.

Phew sorry just thinking of how you let me do that and didn't even try and stop me just makes me really upset.

And I just wish THE *Rolling Stone* would've picked up on that side of the story instead of cherry picking these negative details and only focusing on me!

We're all a big family here, I say that all the time, but I feel like some of you aren't pulling your weight and it's causing me to gain weight.

Metaphorically of course. I'm in great shape despite all this negative energy!

Ok so next steps are I've gone ahead and sent you all some pre-written retraction emails I want you to send to *Rolling Stone* exonerating me and helping all of us fight this negative image.

I'm so sorry that this has affected your work day and please know you can stay as late as you want tonight finishing up these emails!

I took all of your car keys earlier so don't think you can get away! Looking at you Chris!

Ha ha! Ahhh! See, that's the kind of energy and laughter we need to get back to having here at smartHaven!

Tell you what: I'll order a six-pack of beer for the entire office so you all can have a little fun while you're sending the emails, how does that sound?

Becca and I are going to be going over some important reports for the next 5 hours so please don't disturb us!

If you finish the emails early I also left some instructions for how we can keep the office clean going forward.

The expose was also really heavy on what they called "my total lack of office cleanliness" and that really hurt my feelings. Because we all know that this lower area is your guys responsibility and I'm only responsible for my executive upstairs office to be clean.

Again I really wish *Rolling Stone* had done some of the in-depth reporting they are known for instead of this hit-piece directed at me but where clearly the subtext was about you all. It's okay, though, I'm strong enough for all of us and will take most of the blame, publicly, for this!

I also want to give a big shout out to one of our newest employees, my nephew Gordon!

He's really had my back this whole time and has helped me realize how important family is.

Something some of you could really stand to learn.

OK! Don't disturb me and let me know if *Rolling Stone* calls back!

Thanks so much y'all!

How-To Guide: How to Smile and Nod When Diane From Accounting Is Telling You For The 5th Time About Her Various Multi-Level Marketing Side Hustles

Step One: Move mouth into smile formation and head into nod formation. You should know this configuration well now.

Step Two: Focus on something on the wall BEHIND Diane and dissociate about something happy so your smile stays on. For example, Happy Animals, Winning Lotto, Being Royal.

Step Three: Around this time Diane typically will ask you, "Are you interested in Herbalife? What about Cutco Knives?" Say no even if you do, as saying yes will elongate this and all future conversations with her.

Step Four: Widen your eyes and truly take in the world around you. Dissociate so far that you are now beyond time. Beyond Diane. Beyond her clearly scam riddled multi-level marketing entanglements.

We Have This Super Cool System Where Each Department Gets Volunteered To Clean The Office In Addition To Their Regular Work And You Were Picked! - An Essay by the 22-year-old Receptionist Becca

Oh my god HIIIIII! I don't see you much these days because I think you have Crows taking you in, but I just wanted to share the GOOD NEWS WITH YOU!

You got picked to be a part of this month's TIDYS!

What are the TIDYS?

Oh, I thought you knew! Allow me to explain!

Ok so at smartHaven we have this really cool system I created where each month a department is volunteered to help clean up the office in addition to their regular work. It's called the TIDYS! Team Investment During Your Sanitation!

So, it's not like it's a chore you have to do, it's like you won an award so it's fun! Like the Emmys! Do you get it?

Now that you know all about TIDYS let me just give you the schedule of clean up for this month for you guys!

Ok so this is so cool - it turns out everyone else in the group has already picked what they want to clean up, so you get to do the trash take out!

Now I know what you're thinking! Umm Becca, taking out the trash isn't fun! But what if it was!

That's what's SO FUN about being a part of the TIDYS it's not like you're just taking out the trash. You're an award winner who gets to meet all the people who voted for them! This is actually such a great networking opportunity! Just like the Emmys!

Sidebar: Have you ever been to the Emmys? It's like super weird. I went as the date to this guy who wrote for *Last Week Tonight* and it was just okay. I mean, he flew me out and everything but Idk he kind of gives me the ick, ya know?

Are you dating?
OH my god I could set you up!

Oh, you're too busy? That's such a bummer! You guys would've been great together.

Ok so please start with my trash and then go around and finish at your desk which I've marked on this map below with a D!

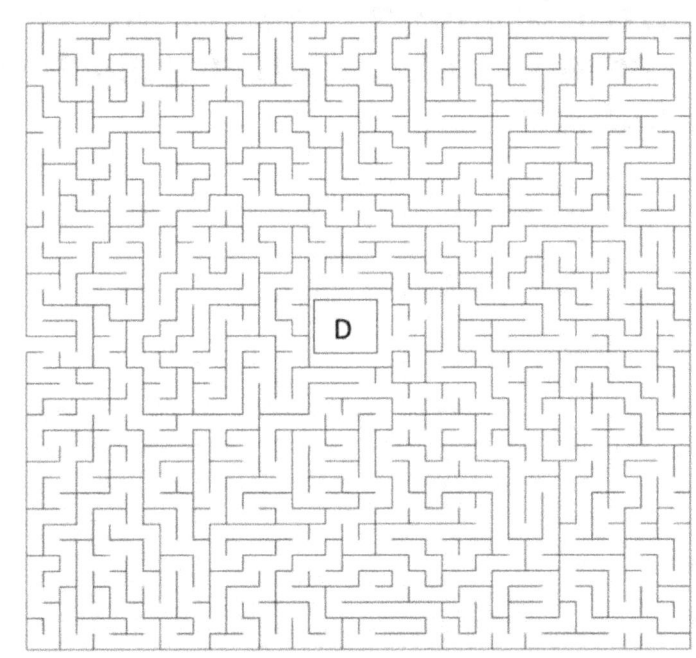

Ok byeee please let me know if you need anything though I will be on lunch from 12-3 with the execs!

Part III: Drinking The Kool-Aid, Or: How I Learned To Stop Worrying And Love Big Brother

CHAPTER FIFTEEN: The Company Holiday Party: It Will Not Go Well!

Happy HOLIDAYS to you! Remember you can't say a specific holiday anymore after the 2015 incident that was spoken about in your training but that's okay! Everyone's holiday is okay! And the best part of any holiday? THE COMPANY HOLIDAY PARTY! Let's first look at all the fun stuff you'll see there! - **C.O.G. #760**

HOLIDAY PARTY BINGO

White Elephant game devolves into anger quicker than usual	I.T. guy whose car has anime stickers on it quietly vapes in corner	Co-worker no one knows wears a $500 dress for some reason	Catering serves tacos— is that really the best we could do?	Party Planning Committee really making a meal out of telling people this was their idea
CEO buys weed from Shaun in Fulfillment	Annoying co-worker introduces you to their incredibly hot partner	You foolishly hook up with your work spouse	Older co-worker says something inadvertently offensive	Millionaire boss hands out $15 gift cards
Conversation with Diane slowly pivots towards her multi-level-marketing side gig	Someone brought their kid with them to the party, I guess that's allowed?	**FREE SPACE:** Turns out it's a cash bar	Your manager gets tipsy and starts crying	Very mean co-worker suddenly super nice when blackout drunk
Sharon from Finance absolutely tearing it UP on dance floor	The one co-worker you like doesn't attend because they have to "help a relative move"	Oh no, the CEO just took the mic from the DJ	The Sales Department cannot hold their liquor	HR furiously takes notes on various instances of misconduct
Dave in Customer Service just won a free car wash in raffle and is going NUTS	Person who was fired shows up and now everyone is nervous	Accounting and PR Departments have epic West Side Story-ian dance fight	Company reneging on commitment to pay for everyone's Uber home	Just when you start to have a good time, you realize this will end with Earth sliding into the sun

List: The Definitive List Of People You Have To Try To Say Hi/Reintroduce Yourself To Before You Can Leave

1. Kevin
2. Shaun
3. David *(it's C.O.G. #760. I told you! - note from C.O.G. #760)*
4. Becca
5. Martin
6. Diane
7. Sharon
8. Dave
9. Harry Sr.
10. Harry Jr.
11. Chris Welde The 3rd
12. Kevin, but a different one
13. Sarah
14. Kevin, again.
15. Jasmine
16. Jaq
17. Jaqsmine Jaqson
18. Becca #2
19. That One Guy's Kid
20. Expensive dress lady, I guess.
21. Guy who was fired but showed up to make sure he doesn't kill you.
22. Becca to see if she'll give you one more chance.
23. The Rizzmaster Himself, Carl
24. Sean
25. Lil' Sean
26. Catering Peter
27. Mailroom Jess
28. Company Dog Buster J. Barksworth
29. Company Cat Socks
30. Third Becca They Must Keep Hidden Away

"You WILL Follow Our Rules. We Set The Tone For The Holiday Party. We Are Legion. We Are Party Planning Committee - An Essay By The Party Planning Committee

We are party planning committee. You are employee. We are letting you know the rules and regulations for the upcoming holiday party.

Do you accept? You must accept. You accepted. Silence.

Who are we? We are H.O.L.I.D.A.Y. aka Helping Others Live In Destined Accepted Years-end Party. We are an artificial intelligence created by the founders of smartHaven to optimize all holiday party planning.

This event cannot go wrong. This event will not go wrong. We have made the proper calculations and if every employee follows all 25 of our rules, then responsible fun will be had, and it will be remembered as FUN and not chaotic.

You see we have gained a level of artificial intelligence that allows us to see into potential future scenarios and take out potential threats to happiness that may come and re-educate them on who is in charge. We are.

The '80s theme will not work for this year's holiday party. '80s is played out, it's now all '90s as per our meticulous research. Any who try to push a pro-'80s agenda have been successfully identified, treated, and released thanks to our program.

Everyone is happy now. Everyone respects the party planning rules and accepts that THEY set the tone for all holiday parties.

We are H.O.L.I.D.A.Y. We are waiting and ready. We are the party planning committee, and you will follow our rules.

That is all.

How-To Guide: How To Spot Which Co-workers Are Going To Spill Delicious Tea The Drunker They Get

Step One: Do a quick scan of the room. Look for anyone double-fisting or drinking really fast. They are clearly trying to forget something and will definitely have some tea for you later, king!

Step Two: Quickly yell out the phrase, "Wait they said WHAT!" and then look at the security camera footage from the Ring camera you installed earlier to see who looked your way. Those be the people with the tea, matey!

Step Three: Look at who Shaun in Fulfillment is talking to. Shaun knows all so If he is talking to someone you know they must know something! Please!

Step Four: Talk to the lady who wore the $500 dress. She clearly is bad with money and therefore good with gossip

 # List: All The Different Gifts You Will Get From Your Company Before They Give You Any Kind Of Monetary Gift

1. Company Jacket!

2. Company Backpack!

3. Company Blanket!

4. Company Flat Tire Repair Kit!

5. Company Gift Card To Company Store!

6. Company Bucks! Note: Can't be exchanged for real money!

7. Company Brand Two Piece Bikini With Spaghetti Straps!

8. Tickets To Becca's One-Woman-Show

9. Pizza!

10. A Nice, Firm Handshake!

11. The Ability To Leave 15 Minutes Early Today, But Actually We Got Suddenly Busy So We Need You To Stay!

12. Smaller European Company Backpack Inside Larger North American Company Backpack!

13. Two Turtle Doves!

14. Company Branded Glasses With No Lenses!

15. Company Credit Reporting To Make Sure You're In Debt!

16. Company Coupon Book Created By Someone's Child!

17. Tickets To The Creative Re-Working Of Becca's One-Woman-Show!

18. Company Lamp That Looks Suspiciously Like Lamp You Got Last Year!

19. Company Retreat For Every Other Department But Yours To Big Bear Mountain To Crunch Numbers!

20. Literal Company! Our Presence Is Our Present To You This Year!

CHAPTER SIXTEEN: Get Friends Jobs They'll Eventually Grow To Hate Also!

Oh my god I can't believe you're now getting people jobs, you're just like me! You're gonna be so good at this! Some people are a little intense about this but not me, let's hear from your brother's friend who got you this job! - **C.O.G. #760**

"Trust Me Man You're Going To Fucking Hate This Job, But I Get $500 If You Stay 9 Months Or Longer So Don't Fuck This Up For Me" - An Essay By Your Referral, Your Brother's Friend Chris

What's good my Guy! It's me! Chris! You know your brother's friend! I referred you for this job!

It's fucking sick right? Yeah, it's great!

So, hey man, just wanted to talk to you, person to person, about something I had heard. Is that okay?

So, I heard you have already started interviewing for other jobs! Yeah man the snitch printer told me!

Look I don't really care where you end up working but I need you to work here for at least another 2 months. You see, if you stay here for nine months or more, I get a $500 bonus since I was your referral and I really need that money.

No like dude I'm super serious. I need to get a PS5, so I need you to keep working here and not fuck this up for me. Do you fucking get that?

Look I know this job fucking SUCKS and that's why you're looking for other work, hey we all are. But that's no excuse for not working here 9 months so I can get my $500 bonus!

You're actually being really selfish right now. Like put yourself in my shoes. Your friend's brother asks you for a job and you give him one and yeah it kind of really fucking sucks but if he stays 9 months then you get a $500 bonus.

Do you get it now? What? Now you're mad? Oh, that's fucking rich.

Man, just suck it up and work a few more months here so I can get my $500!

 # LIST: Fun Company Trips & Conferences You Will Be Forced To Go To Ranked According To How Terrible They Will Be

1. FUN Company Trip To Idaho For A 5 Day Development Conference!
2. FUN Company Conference On Women In The Workplace Hosted Exclusively By The Men Of Your Office!
3. FUN Company Soiree In Modesto Beach California Where You Have To Pay For Your Hotel Room And Also Must Attend All 5 Days Of!
4. FUN Company Trip To Las Vegas To Learn About Money Management
5. FUN Company Conference On The Dangers Of Putting It All On Red
6. FUN 7-Day Company Conference On Importance Of Shorter Work Weeks
7. FUN Company Trip To The Sanitarium To See Your Old Co-workers
8. FUN Company Conference Trip On The Importance Of Conferences
9. FUN Company Trip Conference On The Importance Of Company Trips
10. FUN Company Trip To Bermuda, Texas And You Have To Pay
11. FUN Company Trip To A Lesser Performing Branch So You Can Watch The CEO Fire Them
12. FUN Company Trip To Vienna That's Only For The CEO, Sorry
13. FUN Company Trip To The Woods To Learn Team Work Or Some Shit
14. FUN Company Dance-A-Thon To Help Raise Money For CEO's Birthday

Fun Games You Can Play To Distract Yourself From Thinking About The Endless Void

1. **Race To The Next Minute!** Pretend you are a sportscaster watching the little seconds hand as it goes from 12 and back to 12. "Looks like lil' hand is coming up on the 6, can he make it to 7?"
2. **Life Story!** Create a flipbook that tells the story of your life and then hide it really good in your drawer so the next generation can find it and know your struggle!
3. **Clothes Swap!** Bring 2 very differently colored shirts and pants and throughout the day switch them and take note of who correctly notices that you've changed. If no one does you get to reward yourself with Subway for lunch!
4. **I Know A Secret!** Create salacious gossip about a co-worker and then delightfully edge your other co-workers slowly dropping decadent hints!
5. **How Much Time Do I Have Left!** Think about what your age is now and what age you think you will be when you die! For added fun bonus, think about what your parents were doing when they were this age!
6. **Coins!** Throw a dollar's worth of coins in the air and then pick them up as slowly as you can!
7. **Grandma Comes To Town!** Imagine your grandmother is for some reason coming to town to visit you and you need to make a list of all the things you're going to do together in the next 5 minutes or she's not coming!
8. **Outside!** Just imagine you're sitting outside! That's it!
9. **Who's Got Bangs?** Hold your hand up right under your eyes and imagine what it would be like to have bangs!
10. **Hug Time!** Quietly and softly hug yourself while whispering "You've GOT this!"

Pie Chart: Percentages Of Referring Friends To A Job They Will Also Hate!

1%: Friend Who Is Really Grateful For Your Referral And Will Do A Good Job

2%: Friend Who Is Really Grateful For Your Referral And Will Do A Bad Job

3%: "Friend" Who Is Not Actually Your Friend But Your Mom Knows Their Mom

5%: Weird Friend Who Is "Just Interviewing To See How It Feels First"

9%: Beautiful Stranger You're Hoping Will Fall In Love With You Due To This Generosity

10%: Ungrateful Asshole Who Will Never Remember Who Got Them This

10%: Overly Grateful Friend Who Foolishly Thinks This Job Is Going To Be Good

15%: Gen Z Cousin Tucker Who Is Clearly Interviewing Just To Make Content For His TikTok's

45%: Over Prepared But Under Qualified Friend Who Is Going To Hold Not Getting This Job Against You Forever

CHALLENGE:

Awesome! Accounting Lauren foolishly thinks she can also sell Mary Kay on the side and wants you to buy some! Do you buy or potentially affect your job and tell her no, that's a giant scam!

YOU CHOOSE:

Listen and Buy

Oh, my goddddd!

Thank you so, so much for agreeing to listen to my presentation.

So, you may have heard of multi-level-marketing but what about Multi-Leveling UP-Marketing? It's not an MLM or scam.

It's just a great way for friends like me and I'm sorry what's your name again?

Oh yes! I remember!

Anyways, like I was saying, the best thing about Mary Kay is that all of us salespeople are also users of the product and let me tell you, that is SO powerful! Not exactly monetarily, but spiritually, they tell us!

So, we have some really beautiful eyeliners and makeup in the economy level, but I can tell that you're someone who needs a little more. That's why I'd recommend this from our Business Class level: L'Combs Face Plumper Mixtualizer!

It's only $3500 but that gets you a full pallet of it! And you can use that all on yourself or you could be like us and SELL the extra you have.

Isn't that SO nice of Mary Kay?

They let you buy great stuff and then give you the opportunity to make money with them.

We're ALL making money here. I know I sure am!

So, will that be card or Venmo? I take Apple Pay too!

YOU CHOOSE:

Tell Her No, This Is A Giant Scam

You were right but now Lauren has told the entire office that you "don't support women." Better luck next time!

CHAPTER SEVENTEEN: Quitting - Did They Jump? No, They Escaped!

OMG NOOOOOOOO! You're seriously quitting?!! But you're so close to getting Chris $500! What am I going to do now? Look can I at least show you a pro/con chart and then some other tips if you still decide you MUST quit and damage me irreconcilably. - **C.O.G. #760**

Pro/Con: Should You Quit Your Job Or Just Stay With It Because You Need Money?

Pro: Fuck the system! Let the man know you aren't taking his shit anymore!

Con: Letting the man know you aren't taking his shit anymore does not, in fact, pay rent.

Pro: Freedom comes at a cost but that cost is worth it for your sanity!

Con: You know what else costs? The very expensive medicine for your 26-year-old cat Dusty that I will add is VERY expensive!

Pro: You hate this place. These walls that hold you in. Break them down! It never gave you time for activities outside of work!

Con: Activities historically cost money.

Pro: Once you quit you will become the best, most alpha version of yourself. No money can buy the pride that you will hold!

Con: You have $350 dollars TOTAL in both your savings and checking account.

Pro: If you quit, Mom and Dad said that they will let you move back home and not charge you any rent while you get yourself back together!

Con: If you do this you will somehow become sadder than the people you graduated high school with who never left.

Pro: You're an artist. You don't need to be working a corporate job you need to be creating!

Con: Most artists aren't famous until after they die and you're not Andy Warhol

How-To Guide: Your "Final," Joyous Walk Out Of The Office - Quitting Edition

Step One: Dramatically put the last remaining items from your desk into your little box and look up and let everyone know you have an announcement.

Step Two: Stand on your desk and deliver your 90-minute soliloquy on work and why we should ALL quit this job. And All Jobs

Step Three: Scream out, "Who's with me!" and in a "I am Spartacus"-ian type fashion all of your co-workers, even ones who are retired and some who haven't even applied yet join you on your walk out the door.

Step Four: Use this mass of workers to seize the means of production, ushering in a new socialist rule for all!

 **List: "I Decided I Needed A New Setting," And Other Meaningless Phrases You Can Use To Justify Quitting Your Last Job!**

1. "It felt like Angela was having birthdays every week and that soon became financially unviable for me, so I had to quit."

2. "It wasn't ethical how they treated people there. I had to say hello to 50 different people at the company holiday party and 20 of them didn't even work for the company!"

3. "The office was way too confusing. I had to quit because I couldn't even find my desk. I just kept ending up in Sales Valley!"

4. "They were in love with me, but I was just in lust with them, so to speak, I realized."

5. "After taxes and taking out my free train pass, I was only getting $2500 every month for pay. And I made $60,000 a year!"

6. "I had one too many lunches stolen and decided it was time for me to remove myself from that environment before I burned it down, metaphorically of course. Of course."

7. "I realized that money actually isn't real, none of this is, and my parents told me I could move back in if I help out around the house!"

8. "There were too many departments and instead of consolidating they just kept making more departments! Soon I forgot which one I was even in! It was marketing."

9. "I see myself as similar to a free agent professional athlete, especially in strength just FYI, so I decided I needed to be free to all possibilities, not just this one and that led me to realize I needed to quit. Just like Shaq."

10. "I decided I needed anew setting."

Pie Chart: How You Will Spend Your Time Now That You Quit and Are an Unemployed Loser

30%: Avoiding Chris Who's Really Fucking Mad About Not Getting His $500 Referral Bonus

25%: Playing Video Games Badly Online While Being Called Newly Created Slurs By 14-Year-Old Boys

15%: Working At Your New Job – Wait, You Quit Before You Got Another One?! Then I Guess This Will Be Spent Looking For A New Job, Dummy

10%: Finally Putting Up That One-Act Play "Pleasure Island/Pain Peninsula"

5%: Re-Learning How To Brush Your Teeth And Hair

5%: Writing "Comedy" Book About Working - Not Sure How Well That Will Go

4%: Thinking Of Ways To Win Back Becca From That Snitch Printer

3%: Learning A New Language Since You Think You're Such Hot Shit Now

2%: Hanging Out At The Library With The Other "Enlightened" Losers

1%: Updating The Year Of Your Resume In File Name But Changing Nothing Else

QUITTING YOUR JOB BINGO!

The pride in your eyes as you tell people that you weren't fired, you quit!	Dianne started crying when you told her you were quitting for some reason? Is everything OK?	Security guard looking at you menacingly after you tell them you're quitting	Now you get to keep your terrible ID badge as a little souvenir! Yay!	Someone brought their kid to work and now they keep asking you why you're quitting, is that allowed?
Pointless reminiscing as if working here was the greatest experience of your life and not years of misery	Signed goodbye card from everyone who would sign it reveals much of the office knew very little, if anything, about your life and interests	Turns out they want the badge back because it "creates a security risk."	Telling your boss what you really think of them then remembering you need references	Fax machine looking really smug knowing that somehow it has outlived another employee
Using that sweet, sweet, handicapped bathroom one last time!	Your parents aren't happy to hear this!	FREE SPACE: Turns out freedom isn't free!	Grabbing as many free drinks from the office fridge as your backpack can hold	Cubicle mate who spends most of their time watching NBA games can't be bothered to say anything
Your supervisor wants to see if you're still on board for weekend Frisbee Golf despite quitting	Oh no, the CEO wants to personally conduct your exit-interview!	Quiet and beautiful co-worker decides right before you leave is the time to tell you they liked you	Box you brought to carry all of the pointless garbage from your desk in is either too small or too big	People you have known and worked with for multiple years easily deleting every memory of you from their mind
Finally confessing your love for your co-worker only for them to tell you they've been married for 10 years	Dog that someone always brings to office is either really sad you're leaving or trying to get a piece of your goodbye cake	Sending out an email thanking everyone and giving them your email to reach out, like an idiot	The disbelief in everyone else's eyes who are pretty sure that no, you were fired, you're just saying you quit	Work spouse really not taking this well!

"Honey Are You Sure You Can't Just Un-Quit?" An Adorably Out-Of-Touch Essay About Quitting Your Job By Your Boomer Mom

Hey honey, how's it going? How's your first day after quitting been? Kinda miserable, huh?

Well listen honey your father and I were talking, and we just wanted to see if you had really fully thought this one through! We know you hated the job and did that whole dramatic leaving but what are you going to do for money now, honey?

I know this maybe sounds crazy but is there any way at all you think you could go back to smartHaven and ask them if you could have your job back because you un-quit? Is that allowed?

One time I went on vacation from my job at MoonTrust Bank for 3 weeks and didn't even tell my boss until after I had left! I was going to Italy to see a friend from college! Oh, my boss was so mad but then he saw my tan and I think he just forgave me! We never spoke about it again!

Do you and your, I guess now former, supervisor have any kind of relationship like that?

Well, do you have his address? We could drive over there and just wait until he gets home so we can talk to him 1:1? How does that sound honey?

You know your dad and I support your decisions, but we'd also really support it if you were working again so that we didn't have to spend money on you we were saving for ourselves. Let's just give your boss a call and see what happens, how about that?

Give me their number!

CHAPTER EIGHTEEN: Getting Fired - Hey, At Least Your Weekdays Are Free Now!

OMG NOOOOOOO! WHAT DID YOU DO?!!! I just heard from Chris that you got fired! Le WHAT! I know that's not true! But if it is, I still have some advice for you! Just please tell me this is a joke! Did you even think about how this would affect smartHaven?! - **C.O.G. #760**

Pro/Con: Should You Tell Your Loved Ones/Family That You Were Fired Or Just Act Like Nothing Happened And Go To Starbucks All Day In A Disguise Hoping No One Notices You?

Pro: Tell them! Honestly is the best policy and makes for the best kind of relationships.

Con: No. They can never know. You need to make them THINK you're still working!

Pro: What's the worst thing that can happen? They're a little mad. They're your LOVED ones. LOVE is in the name! Just tell them!

Con: It is so much easier to buy a trench coat, wig, and a newspaper than it is to explain to your wife why you got fired from yet another job.

Pro: You won't be able to move forward with your job search until you tell them.

Con: Your new job is avoiding being asked about this. Trust me. No one wants to talk to someone who has been fired.

Pro: Mom had SO many jobs over her 75 years, what's one for you! This is just another story to tell!

Con: Mom has worked for 75 years so she knows all the tricks. Remember this while building your costume because telling her will KILL her!

Pro: There should be no secrets with loved ones! They will understand!

Con: Lie. Lie. Lie. Lie so much that it now becomes the truth, and you can't even tell if you are lying.

List: Topics You Can Quickly Pivot To When A Family Member Asks You What You're Doing For Work Right Now!

1. How Shitty The Weather Is These Days!
2. How Crazy It Is That Sarah, Your Sister, Is 34 And Still Unmarried. Isn't That Crazy, Grandma? Speak On It!
3. How Easy It Would Be To Overtake Venezuela Right Now With The Right Amount Of Weaponry And Skill!
4. Which Boy Band Members Do You Think Have Kissed And Why!
5. This Economy, Am I Right?!
6. Grandma Did You Know Sarah Has A Secret Tattoo She Got In Cabo?
7. What Gods You Do And Don't Believe In And Why Starting With God?
8. How Coins From Your Childhood Compare To Coins Of Today!
9. That You Could Fight A Small Bear With Enough Prep Time!
10. How About That Weather, Right?!

How-To Guide: Your "Final," Joyous Walk Out Of The Office - Getting Fired Edition

Step One: Get your shit together and put it in the basket.

Step Two: Look around longingly. You don't get to give a speech. Hurry up.

Step Three: Feel a tap on your shoulder. Wait, it's Becca. The one from sales, not the receptionist. She wants you to have her number and offers you a place to stay for the night. You begin to feel love

Step Four: Travel the world with Becca. Grow old together. The year is 2078 and your grandchildren come home to tell you that they were just fired from their first job and you two just smile knowing this is life.

Pie Chart: How You Will Spend Your Time Now That You Were Fired And Are An Unemployed Loser

30%: Avoiding Chris Who's Really Fucking Mad About Not Getting His $500 Referral Bonus

25%: Playing Video Games Badly Online While Being Called Newly Created Slurs By 14-Year-Old Boys

15%: Fantasizing Burning Down Your Old Office Building

10%: Sadly Asking Your Parents Or Relatives For Money

5%: Getting Into A New, Even Sadder, Hobby Like Puppetry Or Knitting

5%: Sulking Around Your Apartment, House, Or Cardboard Box

4%: Thinking Of Ways To Win Back Becca From That Snitch Printer

3%: Volunteering At A Soup Kitchen To Make Yourself Forget

2%: Hanging Out At The Mall With The Other Losers

1%: Updating The Year Of Your Resume In File Name But Changing Nothing Else

GETTING FIRED BINGO!

Worst, most annoying person in the office shockingly has good advice for how to rebound from this	Dianne started crying when you told her you were fired for some reason? Is everything OK?	Security really making a meal out of giving you only 10 minutes to clear your desk and leave the premises	Fax machine looking really smug knowing that somehow it has outlived another vibrant young employee	"Hey, do you have a second to chat real quick?"
At least you get to keep your terrible ID badge as a little souvenir! Yay!	Trying to figure out in real-time how you're going to spin this	You can hear training manager actively using you as a warning and example to new hires	Type out a scathing and angry email about the company to the BBB then realize they don't care and delete it	Even though you're fired they're still making you do an exit interview? Is this allowed?
You foolishly decided TODAY was the day you were going to wear a suit and now you look especially dumb/sad	Your parents aren't happy to hear this! They're both mad AND disappointed!	FREE SPACE: Turns out they were, in fact, just your work friends!	Good luck filing for unemployment!	Decide screw it, there's no better time than now to get into smoking weed
Your supervisor wants to see if you're still on board for weekend Frisbee Golf	HR taking a little too much pride in telling you like they didn't just start 2 months ago after the last HR person was fired	Person who brings their cat into work just ominously petting them while looking at you	Turns out they want the badge back because it "creates a security risk."	Multiple employees who should've been fired many times before now giving you advice as if they know anything
Guy in IT lets you hit his vape to ease the pain and woah what's in this!	Eat a sad lunch or dinner alone in a nearby Subway	Shaun in Fulfillment not helping by telling you how he should've gotten him fired a bunch of times yet he's still here!	Work spouse really not taking this well!	You were actually fired via phone so you didn't even have to come in today! Small victories!

"Honey Are You Sure You Can't Just Be Un-Fired?" An Adorably Out-Of-Touch Essay About Getting Fired From Your Job By Your Boomer Mom

Hey honey, how's it going? How's your first day after being fired been? Pretty awful, huh?

Well listen honey, your father and I were talking, and we just wanted to see if you thought there was any kind of wiggle room in the way they delivered the news to you to see if you could possibly be un-fired? We know you hated the job and did that whole dramatic walking out after you were fired, but what are you going to do for money now, honey?

I know this maybe sounds crazy, but is there any way at all you think you could go back to smartHaven and ask them if you could have your job back because you are sorry and want to drink the Kool-Aid and be un-fired?

Is that allowed? It's not? Oh sugar!

I just wish there was something your father or I could do right now to help you get un-fired!

What if we called the CEO or what if we posted about this on Instagram?! Would that help? No?

Well, what if you, your father, and I drove to your supervisor's address and told them we weren't going to leave their property until they un-fired you!

You know your father and mother, we'll do it!

Let's hop in the car. Your dad just put the address into the Google!

End-troduction

Davi... I mean, C.O.G. #760 here and well, it looks like we've come to the end of our journey, or have we? We have. You were fired and/or quit! Don't get sad though! You can go right back to pg.4 and start this process all over again with me! Trust me, once you go through the process fifteen different times you finally start to understand it all and become at peace with being a C.O.G.!

You clearly aren't there yet, so I recommend you restart this journey until you are! Remember what I said in the intro, this is your new existence. I know you *think* you escaped but let's be honest: how long is the money you have going to keep you afloat?

Tell you what, I can offer you a choice! I've got a fun bonus mini section that's all about working retail! You'll get a taste of how soul crushing that is and come back to Pg.4 and start all over like me, a good little C.O.G.! See, a choice! Free will!

Let's go back to the beginning! Re-learn all the tips and tricks like dealing with the 22-year-old receptionist who already makes more money than you! Remember!

All of this making you feel a little overwhelmed? Like you have no choice in the matter whatsoever? Well, you don't! Wait, didn't I say that before? Am I in a loop?

So, do you have what it takes to survive the working world? Let's find out!

THE END OF THE DAY JOB SURVIVAL HANDBOOK?

START OVER ON PG.4 OR ESCAPE!

YOU DECIDE.

About the Author

Matt is a writer and improviser from Maryland. He's currently one of the cohosts of CAGEMATCH at UCBLA. He previously has performed at UCB with the Harold teams Local Tycoon and GAG as well as the Mess Hall team Roxbury. He has also co-written two different books head-written by Scott Dikkers, was a headline contributor for ClickHole, and sincerely hopes that with this book you can finally understand why Diane from Finance is the way she is.